Footprints of a Shadow

By

Rick Birk

ISBN no. 978-0-9819964-4-8

Library of Congress Categories: Psychology: Sensation.
Consciousness. Cognition. Parapsychology: Sleep.
Dreaming. Visions. Hypnotism. Suggestion. Subliminal
projection. Telepathy. Thought transference. Spiritualism.

This book is easily available at go5books.com

Author's Note

This narrative is based on a true story. The names and some of the events have been altered to protect privacy. To better serve the reader, this book is categorized as "Biographical Fiction." In choosing this classification, the author reveals that *Footprints of a Shadow* contains life experiences as well as certain fictional elements.

Rick Birk

What people are saying about
Footprints of a Shadow

"Jake Connors' quest to understand his haunting, recurrent dream takes readers along with him on his search. His struggle to make sense of the striking dream imagery guides us through various contemporary approaches to dream work. When Jake's dream proves to be largely reality-based, he gets the chance to resolve past grief and embrace life in its surprising richness. Recommended reading on the power of dreams to heal emotional pain."

-Patricia Garfield, Ph.D., author of Creative Dreaming, Co-founder and former President - The International Association for the Study of Dreams

"The prophet Isaiah says: 'Truly, you are a God who hides yourself, O God of Israel, the Savior.' *Footprints of a Shadow* demonstrates beautifully what this means. Through the working of the Holy Spirit, God uses the words and actions as well as the dreams of individual believers to express His infinite love. God grants forgiveness, love, and healing to hearts that have been torn apart through separation from those whom they love. Birk wonderfully reveals in this uplifting book the marvelous attributes of God that are becoming increasingly rare in a selfish and confusing world."

-Pastor David Zimmer - St. Paul's Lutheran Church, McGregor, Iowa

"*Footprints of a Shadow* invites the reader to walk with Jake Connors as he searches for the meaning behind his compelling dream of a past love. Author Rick Birk develops a timeless story which considers the power and meaning of dreams, psychology, spirituality, and romance. This book will encourage the reader to pay attention to dreams and realize that our concept of time may be too narrow."

-Larcy Dunford, MC LPC Therapist - Christian Counseling Center of Scottsdale

What people are saying about
Footprints of a Shadow

"The Universe is very generous when one listens to the messages. The bands of consciousness connect us forever, whether we are in one anothers' lives or not. Even in our limited ideas, we really are connected. These deep soul connections transcend time, space, and limited belief systems. Whether we call it God, Source, or whatever, that deep core connection is the God connection within all of us. When we listen and then act upon the truth, practical, wondrous miracles occur so naturally. A beautiful dream creates a beautiful real experience."

-Sherry Anshara, QuantumPathic Facilitator - Scottsdale, AZ

"Author Rick Birk's novel *Footprints of a Shadow* is a compelling drama about the healing power of dreams. Narrator Jake Connors' quest to uncover his dream's true meaning presents a healing story that is the product of both an open mind and an open heart. It's a story about grief, forgiveness, and real love."

-Michelle Pettit, Library Director - McGregor Public Library

"For anyone who has ever wondered about the transformative effects of their dreams, this book will capture your attention with the engaging narrative of a man who has been touched by a spiritual message in his dreams. Rick Birk takes us along with him on a quest to find the meaning of such a dream and finally to personal wholeness and enlightenment."

-Alyce Tartell, MFA - Holistic Practitioner,
Dream teacher/Consultant - Phoenix, AZ

Acknowledgments

John Birk
Jordan Shoenhair
Alyce Tartell
Tammy Townsend

Dedication

This book is dedicated to my precious wife, Therese. You have not only given me the inspiration to write this story but the courage to search the depths of my being and write with a passion.

I love you,
Rick

Foreword

We will have over 150,000 dreams in our lifetime, and each dream is a complex play of symbolic images and hidden messages. How many of us have had a dream that haunted us and challenged us to find its true meaning? How many of us have wondered if our dreams were messages from across the miles, from across time, or even from departed loved ones?

Throughout the ages, humanity has been fascinated by dreams. Dreaming is an experience common to all people, across all cultures. In ancient Greece and Pharaonic Egypt, dreams were believed to have prophetic qualities. Many Native Americans believe that our dreams reveal the hidden desires of the soul.

In the twentieth century, more scientific information about dreams could be found in such weighty tomes as the *Interpretation of Dreams* by Sigmund Freud. In those days, if a person was interested in having a dream interpreted, he or she might consult a psychiatrist or psychotherapist and be compelled to pay a doctor's fee. Then, in the mid-'70s, Patricia Garfield published her best-seller, *Creative Dreaming*, a book written for the general public. Her book, considered a classic, presented information on dreams in an easy-to-understand format. Finally, we all had the tools to go within to explore our dreams. Dream interpretation had finally entered the mainstream.

Now, in *Footprints of a Shadow*, Rick Birk has taken this one step further, as he gives us an engrossing tale of dreams that both entertains and educates the reader about the meaning of dreams. Throughout this book, we not only learn the answers to questions that are asked in the beginning of the story but gain insight into the richness of the dream world and how we can use this knowledge for our own personal growth and exploration.

For anyone who has ever wondered about the transformative effects of his or her dreams, this book will capture the reader's attention with the engaging narrative of a man who has been touched by a spiritual message in his dreams. The protagonist in this book is an average man who takes a journey into his past and into his subconscious. Rick Birk takes us along with him on a quest to find the meaning of a prophetic dream and, finally, to personal wholeness and enlightenment.

The author has done extensive research on the healing power of dreams and their influence on the human experience. As we follow our protagonist into the world of dreams, we also discover how messages from beyond our physical world are placed into our dreams to help us change and cope with our lives.

-Alyce Tartell, MFA -
Holistic Practitioner, Dream teacher/Consultant - Phoenix, AZ

Prologue

Have you ever had a dream that just seemed real? Did that dream stick in your mind for hours, days, weeks, or longer? Did it tug at your heartstrings with a force so strong that it took over your consciousness? Was it a dream that jumped up and grabbed you and wrestled you into submission? Did it seem more like a revolution than a dream?

If you, too, have experienced such a phenomena, you must wonder why. For all you dreamers out there, heed my words. Do not take these dreams lightly. I am truly convinced that they do in fact have a greater purpose than that of our nightly entertainment. Maybe they are to provide guidance, maybe to calm our wondering minds, or maybe to help us become whole with the grace of God.

Dreams are the door to the light of truth and they do in fact happen for a reason. The truth shall set us free. On February 25, 2009, I ... had such a dream.

Chapter One

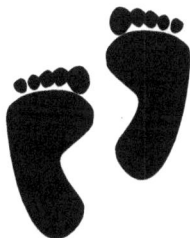

October, 1963

The music from the old record player is ever present in my mind. I still remember the tune, "I want to hold your hand" by the Beatles. A large jack-o-lantern was poised in the corner of the room, a slight flicker emitting from its carved features. Orange and black crepe paper twisted gently, adorning the ceiling, lending ambience to the room. It was the perfect setting for our school's seventh and eighth grade Halloween dance. For weeks the anticipation of this night had been building at our school. 'Trick or treating' would no longer be Halloween's main objective for me. This dance would prove to be my very first social encounter with members of the opposite sex, at the ripe old age of twelve.

All attendees, including several teachers and our principal, were dressed in festive costumes, some cleverly concealing the wearer's true identity. I was dressed like a girl with long dark hair, a pretty dress and makeup. My mother had painstakingly spent more than an hour making my appearance very realistic. In fact, my costume transformation was so professional that my best friend Dave thought I should be seated with the girls on the other side of the room.

The air buzzed with excitement as Mrs. Downey welcomed everyone and announced the first dance. This would be a "boy's choice," she exclaimed. All the boys were seated in chairs against the wall. On the opposite side of the room the girls were similarly posed, anticipating the charge. Once the music started all the boys slowly stood up in unison and, with a little coaxing from Mrs. Downey, ambled towards the girls. For many of us it resembled a walk to the guillotine. As we slowly edged our way to the other side of the room, I knew that I was not the only one hoping that one of our pretty counterparts would give us an encouraging smile. Suddenly a sense of uneasiness took over me and I felt an uncontrollable urge in my stomach. Without warning I began to wretch and vomited all over the floor.

I remember the shrieks and screams of my classmates as the teachers quickly ushered me away. My mother, who had just returned home after dropping me off, was summoned to come right back and pick me up. Unlike me, she seemed to recognize the humor in the situation, apparently understanding the pressure I had been under. This helped to ease my pain just a little.

The following Monday at school proved to be extremely embarrassing. I was razzed by my classmates for weeks. Being a little shyer than most to begin with, I hoped that night would not foretell my future in the world of romance. I remember wondering if the time would ever come when I would feel comfortable with members of the opposite sex.

February, 2009

Living in Arizona had always been a dream of our Connors family. About eighteen years ago, after numerous vacations in the Southwest, we finally made the move. The idea was simple. If we moved from Wisconsin to Scottsdale, Arizona, we would always be on vacation. My wife Julie had found a nursing job at a local hospital and I, Jake, had found a lucrative financial position with an insurance firm. Our two children, Joel and Lucy, acclimated well, making many friends right off the bat. Joel loved the year-around baseball, and Lucy the swimming. Our choice of St. Paul's Lutheran Church was ideal and featured an outstanding youth program. Soon we were able to purchase a home in the McCormick Ranch area, with a pool and several palm trees—a family must. We were living and enjoying the good life. After many years of shoveling snow and raking leaves, we had turned in our shovels and rakes for a pool skimmer and a raft.

By the time they entered high school, the children's interests changed slightly. Joel loved basketball and tennis and was a member of the student council. He received six sports letters in high school and could have competed at a Division III college in either sport. However he decided to give up sports and concentrate solely on academics and devote time to his girlfriend Susan and their future. Lucy, too, loved tennis, but her best sport by far was volleyball. Her team won the state championship her junior year. She also played the clarinet in the school band. Like her brother, she decided not to compete in collegiate athletics. She did, however, want to teach and coach some day.

We loved and enjoyed the kids' high-school years. They had wonderful friends. Our house always seemed to be the meeting place, and we enjoyed hosting many impromptu parties. These were the best of times, and reminded me of my own happy years growing up in Wisconsin.

As a family, we had always displayed a concern for the poor and unfortunate, so one day when Lucy came up with the idea of serving Thanksgiving dinner to the homeless, we all jumped on the bandwagon. For ten years we have met on Thanksgiving day at a homeless shelter in Phoenix to ready and serve dinner to more than 150 individuals. We worked from seven to twelve, which gave us plenty of time for our own family gathering later in the day. The feeling of giving to the community and the unfortunate is something that cannot be duplicated.

College brought changes. Both children opted to stay close to home, and went on to complete their college degrees at Arizona State University, each graduating with honors, which made Julie and I typically proud parents. Both went on to careers they had a passion for—Joel went into finance and Lucy into teaching. Immediately both talked about getting a master's degree. A few years later Joel received his MBA from Arizona State and was ready and determined to take on the world. With his education completed, Joel asked Susan, his lifetime love, to become his wife. It was a spectacular wedding that brought tears to our eyes.

Lucy had not yet found her soul mate, but her career as a teacher and coach was flourishing. She intended to start her master's degree in the fall. We prayed that someday she would meet the right person to share her life. Empty nesters at ages 57 and 58, Julie and I were preparing for our golden years, which we hoped would arrive in the next three to four years. Our family had always put emphasis on nutrition and physical fitness and Julie and I were in excellent health. My only complaint–a bothersome knee due to an old college basketball injury.

In the last year and a half the economy took a huge turn for the worst. President Obama had recently been elected and the country seemed to be hoping for a ray of light. Up to this point in time, the only financial problems our family had been affected by was the bursting of the tech bubble in 2000. Since then we had done well and kept ourselves safe and diversified. Nonetheless the financial meltdown had left a deep scar on America. This was an extremely trying time for most Americans. It was a time of uncertainty and a time to make astute financial decisions. Oil prices were fluctuating like a yo-yo. Many banks went under due to the sub-prime crisis and it seemed that almost every day you would hear of a business laying off thousands of workers. It appeared that businesses were not taking any chances and reacting very quickly in an effort to streamline their human capital. The first bailout by the federal government seemed to have little to no effect on the economy. Many felt its impact, if any, was undetectable.

Neighborhoods were being torn apart in an unpredictable manner. Home values declined sharply and foreclosures popped up on a daily basis. If a neighborhood suffered such a foreclosure, the home values of the remaining homeowners were significantly reduced. New horror stories surfaced each and every day. Someone could be living the good life only to learn that a neighbor may have lost his job and faced foreclosure. If you had a job and planned to stay in your home indefinitely, this economic situation might be easier to bear. The uncertainty was scary. To add fuel to the fire, the Madoff scandal had recently surfaced indicating investor fraud. The losses from the alleged Ponzi scheme were estimated to be between fifteen to twenty billion dollars. Many of the investors were very prominent people. Many wondered when the next shoe would drop.

Fortunately for me, I worked for a private consulting firm that was virtually recession proof. The company managed insurance rehabilitation, liquidation and receiverships. After being awarded a company as a fiduciary of the court, we worked to preserve and protect the integrity and assets of the company as well as maintain the income stream. Our pro-active approach provided a necessary service. We aided companies that were in dire need of solid financial management expertise as well as some already in the depths of despair–ones who were already completely upside down. Each day the list of our potential clients seemed to grow exponentially.

Julie, my wife of thirty-six years, was also in a relatively secure profession, nursing. Additionally, she had years of seniority. We felt very blessed to have job security especially in this economic downturn.

In late February, several of my work colleagues and I

attended an economic forecast seminar in Phoenix. Scottsdale Bank sponsored the event which was held at the Ritz Carlton Hotel in the Biltmore area. Ben, my work buddy, and I drove together from our corporate office in Scottsdale. The program featured speakers in the areas of economics, banking, real estate and securities, and was divided into four general areas. The seminar began with a macro view of the economic forecast in the U.S. as a whole, then narrowed the forecast to the Western region, one that would have a greater impact on the regional audience in attendance. Thirdly, they talked about the financial markets and finally, real estate and construction. No matter how charismatic the speaker, the meeting had an overwhelming aura of doom and gloom. As my colleague Ben said—"Geez, I feel like I'm at a funeral and should be sizing up my own casket!"

John Lewis, a speaker from a local brokerage firm, initially told the audience that there were signs indicating that the financial meltdown was starting to stabilize. That comment, however, was short lived as he seemed to be swept into the mood of the day and found himself quickly retracting that opening line. He told us that large swings in the equities markets would now be commonplace and people should react accordingly. Again people should not put all their eggs in one basket and stay diversified. He went on to say that one of the biggest hurdles seemed to be the potential for more and more firms to fail not only in our region, but nationwide. He noted that companies appeared to be reacting very quickly to our faltering economy. He had never seen anything like it, as employers were very quick to reduce their work force. Massive layoffs by what had appeared to be the most stable of companies had certainly tarnished the landscape. As a result, the first place companies identified for cost savings was in the area of labor and attributable expenses. This produced diminished or reduced incomes for families and led to declining consumer spending. A global downturn was now quite evident and America's affect on the world markets was extremely significant, more than people truly realized.

Yes, the world was now a global economy, he said. The tight credit markets made it difficult for businesses and individuals to secure credit dollars needed to make ends meet. He felt that a very deep recession was possible, but not probable. Even though the federal government had lowered the fund rate many, many times, it had not produced the liquidity in the system needed to generate a positive response. All and all, the confidence of the American people was at an all time low. Everyone needed to adjust and learn how to live in these challenging, difficult times. Individually, they needed to cut back their spending. However, with less restaurant visits, fewer new clothes and the unrealistic probability of a new car, businesses would be placed in their defensive mode and react accordingly.

Mr. Lewis closed on what appeared to be the theme of the day. "After all," he stated, "Even the President has announced, 'The party's over.'"

With that he left the podium to a less-than-enthusiastic round of applause. Again Ben chimed in, "What was his name again—Mr. Warmth?"

The Master of Ceremonies returned to the podium to introduce the last speaker—a surprise guest named Cynthia Tarver, a "Holistic Health Educator, Dream Consultant, and Predictor of the Future." It seemed unusual. A ... holistic practitioner? Tongue in cheek, I mentioned to Ben—"You mean, it really *has* come down to this–we all need to get in touch with our feelings?"

Ms. Tarver reviewed her background, which included psychology, Reiki, energy, healing, dreams and metaphysics. She had been a frequent guest on local radio and television shows and her ability to predict the future and analyze dreams was well documented. She seemed to speak from her heart and left us with a great deal to think about. She emphasized the power of positive thinking and even suggested that we consider meditation to be incorporated into our prayers on a daily basis. She said that if you worry too much, you are using your faith in the wrong direction. There will be good days ahead. God can do the impossible and we must trust in Him. We must prepare ourselves and be ready when opportunities arise.

Her predictions of our tenuous economy did however seem more favorable than that of 'Mr. Warmth.' Regardless, it seemed to me that many of her suggestions and thoughts were much too broad and vague and very simply could be attached to almost any economic scenario. My conservative, detail-oriented background would not allow me to simply accept her outlook and suggestions as simply 'the gospel' or even a slight probability. Near the end of her talk, Ms. Tarver referred to a prayer from the Bible—Job 33: 14-18:

For God may speak in one way or in another, yet man does not perceive it. In a dream in a vision of the night, when deep sleep falls upon men, While slumbering on their beds, Then he opens the ears of men, and seals their instruction. In order to turn man from his deeds, and conceal pride from man, He keeps back his soul from the pit, and his life from perishing by the sword.

Ms. Tarver went on to say, "We all dream, and if we do not understand these dreams, don't worry. The Lord will make sure that we understand just enough, and He will simply take care of the rest." She finished with the following statement. "Ladies and gentlemen, think thoughts you want to happen. Take notice of your thoughts and dreams, as they are truly the door to the future. Knock and it will be opened to you. And always remember, things truly do in fact happen for a reason."

Ms. Tarver left the podium to a very healthy round of applause, even though many had left early, not giving her remarks any credibility. The emcee retook the podium to announce the door prizes for the day. Some nice prizes, including several gift certificates were announced. I was utterly surprised to hear my ticket number called for the next prize–a complimentary one-hour dream interpretation with Ms. Tarver, a $60 value.

Ben quickly jumped in, "Hey, wait until she hears about Marcy in accounts payable!"

I said, "No, Ben, that's your dream. My dream is waiting for me at home!" I took the coupon and put it in my briefcase. I had no dreams to speak of or at least that I could remember. I thought I might give it away to someone who might better appreciate its value.

Chapter Two

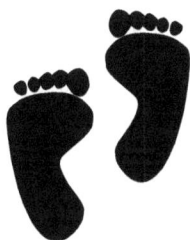

A rriving home, I was exhausted. Julie, as always, was there to greet me with a big hug and kiss. That always made any trying day much better. Over dinner that night, I shared the day's seminar. I described the doom and gloom message re-echoed all afternoon by each of the speakers. She laughed when I mentioned that the meeting concluded with a presentation from a "holistic practitioner." She quickly added, "Really, Jake, that's not a bad thing. Even at the hospital we are getting away from traditional western medicine and taking more of a holistic approach to many issues. It is the up and coming wave of the future. Personally, I am excited about it and you know that my Reiki class falls within this parameter."

Julie always had a way of making sense of even the strangest of issues. We retired that night without any mention of the door prize I had won.

The next morning I woke in deep thought. Strangely for a non-dreamer, I had experienced a dream and was starting to remember fragments of it. A short time later the clock went off. Julie moved closer to give me a hug. To my initial lack of response she asked, "Honey—is everything O.K.?"

"Not really. You won't believe this, but I had a dream."

Julie laughed. "I guess you had too much of the holistic approach yesterday! Please tell me about your dream."

"O.K., but it is a little weird."

As I spoke, the dream easily unraveled from my unconscious. I then began to relate my dream and gave Julie the following account.

"I am seated at a picnic table in a beautiful park-like setting on a sunny spring afternoon in the Midwest. Seated at my right is Carol, my high-school girlfriend from thirty-eight years ago. We are now married to other people. I ask her how many children she has. She answers three. I tell her that I have two. She looks at me, smiles, and then stands up. She says, 'Jake–would you attend a church retreat with me?' She turns to walk down a path toward the forest. Suddenly I see a man seated across from me. He is handsome with a dark complexion, dark hair, and neat goatee. He says, 'Carol is having some major problems and she really needs your help.' Somehow I had the feeling they were psychological issues. He continued, 'Will you help her?' Then I woke up."

I looked oddly to Julie for a response.

"Wow, that does seem a little weird—especially since you remember the dream in such detail."

"It seemed so vivid! That's never happened to me before. It was like I was right there, living the moment," I replied.

Neither of us discussed the dream any further that morning, but I think it was on both our minds. It certainly was on mine.

That day at work I had difficulty concentrating. No matter what task I worked on, the dream seemed to take over my thought process and continued to come right back to me. Never before had I experienced such a vivid dream, much less a phenomenon. The dream brought me back to a time in my life some thirty-eight years earlier in the late 1960's. I had lived in a small town in southern Wisconsin. It had been a wonderful childhood and Carol had not only been my girlfriend, but my best friend for nearly three years.

I arrived home for the evening with the dream still on my mind. I mentioned this to Julie.

"Boy, this thing has really sent you for a loop, hasn't it?"

"I just can't get it out of my mind," I replied.

"It may be some type of warning or maybe you are having a midlife crisis!"

After dinner, Julie was thumbing through a flyer from the local junior college and exclaimed, "Jake!"

I turned to her, and she smiled as if she were a cat that had come upon a canary. "The schedule this semester offers a two-week 'Interpreting Your Dreams' class on Tuesday and Thursday nights from seven to nine p.m. It's scheduled to start this Tuesday. You should sign up."

"Going back to school at my age–are you serious?"

"It's only four times. Who knows? Maybe we could learn something. I dream, too, and I'd love to hear what a college teacher would have to say on the subject. You go and we can share the information without both of us paying to attend."

"I guess maybe I could. To get this thing cleared up once and for all? Let me think about it until tomorrow."

I had the same dream that night, this time even more intense. All day at work it was on my mind. That night I decided to call the local junior college and was pleased to hear that the class was still open. I was advised, per the instructor's recommendation, to bring a dream to class to discuss. I told the registrar that it would definitely not be a problem.

By Tuesday I was still haunted by the dream. I was starting to get headaches, and my sleep and work were suffering. Would this class be able to provide me with some quick answers? In preparation for class, I had typed up my dream and had looked up its symbols in an old dream-symbol book we had lying around. I would tackle this thing head on. This dream had attached to me like a cast one must wear for a length of time to again become healthy. This dream had taken over me. Were feelings for Carol resurfacing after all this time? It certainly wouldn't be fair to my wife Julie.

Did I still love Carol or was there still unresolved business? Was she in need of help? It didn't seem healthy and productive to look back some thirty-eight years. Not only was the dream constantly on my mind, but it was serving to rekindle thoughts of the past, things that I had not thought of for a long, long time. These thoughts seemed to be getting clearer and clearer with the passing of each and every day. I was in dire need of an answer.

Tuesday night was approaching. I could hardly wait. Hopefully I would get the answers I needed and I could finally put this thing to rest. I was starting to view this dream as if it were a term paper. A paper I needed to get an A on just to keep my sanity.

At class that night as I took my seat, I couldn't help notice that there were only six people in the class. Mrs. Evans, the instructor, thumbed through her paperwork and announced that we would begin in a few moments. As I further surveyed the room I couldn't help but notice that all my classmates were women. I was in a room completely filled with women, at a desperate time in my life. Would my feminine side surface?

Class began. Mrs. Evans introduced herself and explained that she had taught this class for more than thirty years. She mentioned that we would need to acquire a book for the class called *Creative Dreaming* by Patricia Garfield. She turned to a quote she had written on the white board just behind her. "Please read this quote by Charles F. Haanel carefully–it's extremely important."

I read: *A recognition and understanding of the resources of the subconscious mind will indicate that the only difference between the subconscious and the universal is one of degree. They differ only as a drop of water differs from the ocean. They are the same in kind and quality, the difference is one of degree only.*

She then pointed to the other side of the board, to another quote. "When you are finished with the first quote read this second quote, by Patanjali. These two quotes are very dear to me and set the stage for the expectations of this class."

When you are inspired by some great purpose, some extraordinary project, your thoughts break their bonds. Your mind transcends limitations. Your consciousness expands in every direction. You find yourself in a new, great, and wonderful world. Dormant forces, faculties and talents come alive. You discover yourself a greater person by far than you ever dreamed yourself to be.

She looked to us, and officially began.

"Ladies and gentleman, by confronting our dreams we can readily deal with precisely where problems start, in our minds. We sleep a third of our lives. Everyone dreams—even animals. Hippocrates, the father of medicine, believed that our souls receive messages during the daytime and at night generate these same images. We must allow them to let us learn and grow. The power of suggestion is prevalent when it comes to dreams. As we fall asleep, we must suggest to ourselves to remember our dreams. It has been proven that when a person takes a nap it is many times more likely that they will retain their dream. Many people don't remember their dreams because they do not wish to deal with issues at hand. Our souls can basically take any and all information from our daily thoughts and experiences and incorporate them into our dreams.

Dreams are messages that come from our inner self and can benefit us immensely. Because of the way the mind works, these messages come in the form of symbols. We have approximately four to five dreams a night, and they probably last for an hour to an hour and a half. We must learn to eliminate the dreams that create fear in our minds and try to produce dreams that we truly want and desire. The purpose of dreaming is not just for own nightly entertainment. Dreams can provide guidance, or relate to what's been on our mind. Dreams can be a warning, and may refer to unfinished business, or may even be a prophetic message. If the dream is prophetic, it will usually manifest itself within the next month. A déjà vu experience is a prime example.

Dreams can be any number of things and are uniquely significant to each individual. Dreams can improve one's health and help a person sleep better. Jack Nicholas, the famed golfer, once was having an issue with his golf swing. He dreamed one night of a new way to hold his golf club. Implementing this newfound method the next day, he went on to correct his swing and met with great success. One member of the singing group the Beatles, Paul McCartney, was said to have discovered a song or two from dreams. We all know the story of the birth of Jesus and the three kings that presented Him with gifts of gold, frankincense, and myrrh. If you remember, the three kings were requested to return to Herod after their stop in Bethlehem. However, they were warned in a incredible dream not to return to see Herod, as it would be unsafe. With this newfound knowledge, they safely returned to their own country.

There are many other biblical references to dreams. Joseph, son of Jacob, had a rare ability to interpret dreams. As a young man he was cast into slavery by his half-brothers. In prison, he interpreted the dreams of two of the Pharaoh's former officers. Both interpretations came true. Later when one of these two men was freed and again working for the Pharaoh, he related the story to the Pharaoh who had actually had two very troubling dreams himself. The Pharaoh had been looking for someone to help him interpret the true meaning of his dreams. Joseph was chosen and once again was able to successfully interpret the Pharaoh's dream. Joseph later predicted seven years of abundance followed by seven years of famine. As a result, Joseph convinced the Pharaoh to store one-fifth of each of his crops in the good years in order to have enough supply to make it through the years of famine.

Another famous musician, Frederic Handel, who composed the exquisite Messiah, was said by many to be in a dream-inspired state for some three weeks prior to its completion. It was said that this state of mind allowed him to create this magnificent work.

Ladies and gentleman, we must pay attention to our dreams and the symbols they do in fact present. Our subconscious speaks to us with these symbols. Dreams are our personal expressions of thought and we should all strive for dream recall. This course is designed to help you to remember your dreams, cope with fear, understand yourself and receive answers to your everyday problems. There is a universal stream of thought in the cosmos ready for our communication."

She added that through the years her understanding of dream interpretation has changed from her experiences. She went on to infer that there are two possible sources of our dreams. "These dreams are either from God or from us," she stated.

She then asked the class, "How many of you dream in color?"

Only two raised our hands, the woman on my right and me. She smiled.

"Many people believe that black and white dreams are just simply dreams while dreams that are in color are actually dreams that have a similar experience in real life," she explained. "People also say that black and white dreams refer to a set of circumstances in the distant future, whereas colored dreams indicate that the dreams are coming closer to reality. I also want to mention that if the same dream happens over and over again—a recurring dream—it could be a warning of some sort."

She smiled again. "Okay, before we get too much further, I would like a volunteer to tell their dream to the class."

I quickly raised my hand, and she nodded. She scanned her list of students, and said, "Jake is it?"

"Yes, I—have it all typed up for you."

"Wow, you are really prepared. Please begin."

I took a deep breath, and stood. I seemed a bit emotional at the thought of having others hear my personal thoughts, but quickly brushed the thought aside and began:

"I am seated at a picnic table in a beautiful park-like setting on a sunny spring afternoon in the Midwest. Seated at my right is Carol, my high-school girlfriend from thirty-eight years ago. We are now married to other people. I ask her how many children she has. She answers three. I tell her that I have two. She looks at me, smiles, and then stands up. She says, 'Jake–would you attend a church retreat with me?' She turns to walk down a path toward the forest. Suddenly I see a man seated across from me. He is handsome with a dark complexion, dark hair, and neat goatee. He says, 'Carol is having some major problems and she really needs your help.' Somehow I had the feeling they were psychological issues. He continued, 'Will you help her?' Then I woke up."

Mrs. Evans nodded. "That's a pretty interesting dream. The features you describe are very detailed."

"I usually don't remember my dreams, but on this occasion I felt that I was right there participating—just as if I were awake," I added.

I then offered to show her the analysis I had done using an old dream book.

"Please do–let's give that a shot."

I began. "I took all the symbols in the dream and looked them up for possible meaning. The sight of a friend in distress could mean that sickness or trouble is around them. Maybe it is a call for help. If you meet a dark character that you don't know, this could represent the masculine side of my personality. It could represent unfinished issues that need reconciliation. If the person is handsome, they have to do with action, conviction and assertiveness. Maybe it's the heroic part of us that wants to surface. The park is a place of enjoyable leisure and a place of wish fulfillment. A picnic refers to rest and relaxation. The table symbolizes happy reunions and prosperous circumstances in our lives. A church retreat can symbolize my lack of spirituality and suggest that I attend to this need. The path that Carol takes could be an emotional journey, an unknown path, and could possibly represent a new direction in my life. A sunny day suggests optimism and well-being. The forest symbolizes darkness and mystery and the unknown. Finally, the spring represents new beginnings, rebirth, youth, and first loves. It could refer to a new project in my life. Maybe hardships I have encountered will somehow lead to success."

"Great job, Jake! I commend you for your efforts. Class—does anyone have any comments about this analysis?"

Not a hand went up.

It was then that Mrs. Evans made a point that seemed to make a great deal of sense. "We need to interpret our dreams using our very own personal symbols," she explained. "Very simply, if you experience a dream that is not within the language of your mind, you will not be able to understand and remember it. Symbols are unique. No book can accurately list any one person's individual symbols. What a symbol means to one person can mean completely the opposite to another. I didn't stop you on purpose for this reason. Let me give you an example. Having a special uplifting dream on the nineteenth of a month may be a positive sign for a person because they were born on the nineteenth and their wedding anniversary was on the nineteenth. However, if on that same day of the month you had experienced a significant loss such as your mother's death or had miscarried a baby, you might feel quite the opposite."

We spent the rest of the evening going around the room, giving everyone a chance to share their dream. People readily shared their dreams, but most offered little or no analysis. However, Mrs. Evans interjected insight by sharing her perceptions of the dreams and offered possible alternatives for our consideration. She made sure that ample time was spent on each person's dream. Hearing everyone's dreams made me feel a little more secure knowing I wasn't the only person with a dream issue.

The evening flew by quickly. Our teacher suggested that we all get a good start reading *Creative Dreaming*, and then ended the class with these thoughts. "We only use ten percent of our brains, so the rest is there to communicate with the universal stream of thought. Sure, some symbols are relatively general, but remember that we must learn to interpret our dreams on what we feel is right—not what someone suggests a symbol stands for. As you become more adept at the process, you will be able to pick up the meaning of the symbols and understand which dreams are, in fact, significant."

Chapter Three

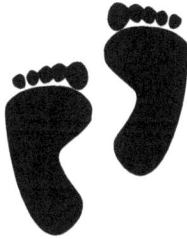

A rriving home I was excited to share what I had learned in my dream class with Julie. There she was sitting on the couch, that big smile and curious look spread across her face. I sat down next to her and we went over my notes in detail. I told Julie that I was a little embarrassed with my presentation and the analysis of my dream and explained to her what had transpired.

"Honey, it's a learning experience," she advised. "I wouldn't worry about it." Yet, for the next few days the dream was still lingering, still giving me a headache. At night I would lie awake for hours thinking about it.

Thursday soon came. Almost everyone had made significant progress reading the assigned book. Mrs. Evans was pleased with everyone's work and stated that she could see that this was one of her more mature classes. Then she began her lecture.

"As we sleep," she told us, "our brains work through our daily encounters. In other words, the brain is constantly at work during our lives. There are five stages of sleep. We actually go from very light sleep in level one and progress to a deeper sleep in level four. It is in level four that we are able to begin to have rapid eye movement (REM). Level five is full REM, and it is in this stage, that we are in a near paralyzed position, and most dreams occur."

She talked about the importance of dreams within cultures. In prehistoric times dreams were recorded on cave walls. American Indians ascribed great importance to dreams. They felt that great symbols and messages obtained from dreams carried over to their waking life. These dreams taught them many things, such as problem-solving, and gave them encouragement and hope. Additionally, these dreams were the hidden desires of the soul and communication from spirits above. The Bible, too, has many references to dreams and people's abilities to hear the word of God through our dreams. The Romans believed that dreams were messages from the gods. Emperor Augustus ruled that any dream a person had about the state must be announced in the marketplace.

To induce dreaming, Mrs. Evans recommended that we attempt to incubate our dreams. The ideal time would be when we go to sleep just before entering our hypnotic-like state. During this time, we were encouraged to attempt to script or set the stage for our dreams. "Summon your inner resources," she encouraged us. "The result may be a major break-through and offer you new, clear insight to anything from seemingly insignificant dreams to very significant dreams related to potential career opportunities, creative ideas or new inventions. Repeat to yourselves, 'I want to remember my dreams,' and even request to dream about a specific person or circumstance."

Mrs. Evans shared that dream incubation started in Egypt, where they recorded their dreams on papyrus. Incubation had been very important to the Greek civilization, and the Chinese were said to practice dream incubation in special dream temples. To aid us, she recommended that we keep a dream journal or tape recorder readily available so that we could easily record our dream at a moment's notice. We were informed of the importance of lying still once we woke up. She believed that because of the lactic acid in the body, movement would make the dream escape more readily from our memory. She wanted us to progress and be able to find ourselves in the state of just having dreamed and seize the moment. We were encouraged to quickly try to get back into the dream and recreate it, almost as if we were trying to reel in a fish on the end of a line.

The ability to have a lucid dream was somewhat advanced. Here the dreamer would have greater control with the dream. If successful, she suggested that we set up a preconceived signal with our minds, such as tugging at our ears to remind ourselves that we are actually in a dream. Then our minds would realize what is actually happening and allow us to interact freely. In these lucid dreams, one would be able to have improved recall and possibly direct the action and dialogue.

A week later, in our third class, we delved into the theories of the Gestalt. Gestalt psychology had its beginning in the late 1800s, introduced by Austrian philosopher Christian von Ehrenfels. In this theory one would use his dream as a basis to examine himself. Our subconscious desires are ones that we are unaware of in our waking lives but may surface in our dreams. This theory holds that the elements in the dream are the parts of ourselves that need to be evaluated. Gestalt theory can erase mental blocks we have built up and lead to self-discovery.

Analysis, she told us, can be good or bad depending on our interpretation. This method of evaluating the dream is sometimes referred to as "Gestalting the Dream." Each element of the dream is a part of the person, who acts out all of the dream's aspects. In other words, a person could be a table, an animal, a car, or another person. He simply needs to somehow have a conversation with the persons or objects in the dream and learn from these dialogues the message he is to receive.

This prompted a lively class discussion. How could we accomplish this? Mrs. Evans suggested, "A person needs to set up a dialog with the particular aspect of the dream and build a scenario that might include the exchange of a present or gift. This present or gift would then contain the message."

As we talked about the Gestalt theory I couldn't help but think about the many elements of my dream. For a person who still couldn't remember his dreams, it was probably a considerable long shot to even consider this theory in my regard.

On the fourth and final evening we learned about what the teacher called the *Shadow Self*. Here both our conscious and unconscious minds create our future. There are both good and bad aspects of our unconscious mind that exist on many levels. For the most part the undesirable parts are referred to as "Your Shadow Self." A person using Gestalt theory must get to know his Shadow Self in order to make self-improvements. She felt that our conscious mind was for the most part unaware of the Shadow Self and its less than admirable aspects that exist at our lowest levels, where our fears reside. If a person harbors resentment for having been rejected in a former relationship, it might exist at this level. If you are jealous of a co-worker's advancement, it could be located here. If a person in your dream was acting in a negative way, this may be an indication of the behavior one needs to work on.

As we talked about this new element, the Shadow Self, I grew intrigued. Already I was starting to formulate a new meaning for my recurring dream. After all, wasn't this the objective for taking this class? Basically, I needed to resolve this thing in some way. I was having little success in having another dream, much less in communicating with a participant in my original dream. Up to this point in my life I had put little credibility in dreams, especially with my conservative background and on occasion my "anal-retentive" approach to life. I now felt strongly that my dream had little if anything to do with my relationship to Carol, my former girlfriend. I had considered that, because she had been my first love, I could still be infatuated with her. I hadn't thought about her in years. It simply made no sense. Why would a person want to go back and dig up old thoughts and feelings? What would there be to gain? In my estimation this would defy logic. I loved my wife Julie very much. Possibly I was sad to say good-bye to my childhood at one time. Besides, it seemed a little far-fetched that Carol did in fact need help.

Somehow this dream *had* to do with that man on the other

side of the picnic table. After all, he had a dark complexion and dark hair, a shadowy image. It must be some aspect of my Shadow Self that I needed to come to grips with. And he had made the effort to communicate with me. Who was that man? What, in fact, did he represent to me? What was he trying to impart? I could think of no reason. This figure, however, had been if anything, very cordial to me and in no way had seemed to have any flaws in his personality that would identify with a negative quality. Unlike the others in the class, my key problem was my inability to find a way to contact that man.

This fourth and final night left me somewhat depressed. It seemed everyone but me had made significant progress. Some of the women were remembering everything in their dreams. Some were even to the point of participating in lucid dreams. I had started the class the first night with what I thought was a home run, but my batting average seemed to be slipping more each session. I now couldn't get to first base, and the dream was still giving me grief each and every day. I wondered if maybe women have an easier time communicating, or getting in touch with, their inner self. But I didn't dare bring this up in the class.

With thirty minutes left in class, Judy, seated to my right, asked Mrs. Evans a very intriguing question. "Could a person use a dream to contact an individual who had passed away?" The question surprised everyone, including Mrs. Evans. The class sat in silence as she carefully explained that she did not want to delve into this aspect now, but would answer the question at the end of class.

As the class ended, my classmates and I said our goodbyes. Mrs. Evans smiled and told me not to worry. The answer would soon come to me, if I remained diligent. I thanked her for all her efforts. As I left the room, I noticed Mrs. Evans and Judy were the only ones left, in a deep discussion. I found myself wondering about the answer to Judy's question.

At home, I again reviewed my notes and shared my progress with Julie along with my final analysis and insight regarding my dream.

"Honey, I think the dream is somehow related to my shadow self. I truly feel that I am, or need to be, transformed in some way—and maybe it'll lead to my growth as a person."

She smiled. "I just wish you could talk to that guy at the picnic table. It sounds like he's the one with all the answers!"

I had a restless night. The dream was still etched in my mind. I seemed to sleep so lightly, never achieving the deep slumber I was normally accustomed to weeks before. The next day several people at work even remarked how tired I looked. About noon, I hunkered down in my office to catch a quick bite to eat. Julie called shortly after, to see how I was doing. I told her I was hanging in there, and I appreciated her concern. She said that if I didn't get over this soon she might have to get me something temporary to help me sleep. She reminded me to pick up some milk and butter on the way home.

I scrawled a quick note and hung up. I reached over to put the note in my briefcase, sitting on my credenza. As I reached over I knocked over my briefcase. Its contents spilled on the floor. As I began to clean up I noticed the coupon—the door prize I had won at the conference. I had forgotten all about it. It was for the one-hour session with Ms. Tarver, the holistic practitioner and dream analyst. I thought about it for a second. Maybe, just maybe, this woman of renown fame could help me. After all, she was one of the best in the business.

I scanned the card for her number, jumped up and closed the door to my office. I made the call, and to my surprise, Ms. Tarver answered the phone. I told her about the seminar and how I had gotten her name. I gave her some background and told her about my problem. She was very cordial. I was elated when she told me that she had a cancellation at five-thirty that evening. She proceeded to give me directions to her home in south Scottsdale. She thanked me for calling and said she looked forward to meeting me.

I called Julie and told her about the door prize and my appointment. I could tell by the excitement in her voice that she could hardly wait to hear the result. I said a quick prayer that Ms. Tarver could help me. I was hopeful that she would help me unlock the mystery. I prayed that she would be able to provide me with some insight and answers. I was optimistic that she could not only help me understand the significance of the dream but also discover the identity of the man on the other side of the picnic table and his intentions for me.

The afternoon crawled by. I could hardly wait. At precisely five o'clock, I was out the door, ready to take my next step in what by this time seemed to be more of an adventure than a dream.

Chapter Four

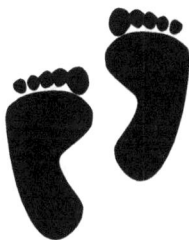

As I made my way down Hayden Road, I felt nervous and apprehensive. How ironic, I thought. Only weeks before at the seminar, I remembered winning the gift certificate, a one hour consultation from Ms. Tarver. At the time, I thought it was highly improbable that I would ever use the gift certificate. Now, here I was, looking forward to my consultation. I was looking to her to free me from what I nearly believed was a spell. My perception of dreaming and its effects had changed—radically—in just a few short weeks.

I arrived at the south Scottsdale location. There sat a modest stucco home with a tile roof on a relatively small lot. Several angel statues stood in the front yard. Chimes pended on the front porch. I rang the doorbell. Ms. Tarver responded quickly with her signature smile. She welcomed me, and shook my hand firmly.

"It is very nice to meet you Jake."

"I appreciate you seeing me on such short notice," I replied. An odor hung in the air. I quickly discovered the source. Two cats were prowling around.

"Right this way, Jake. Don't worry about Oscar and Felix–they're both harmless."

One cat was much larger than the other. One was black, the other ginger. They did resemble an odd couple—hence, their names.

Ms.Tarver ushered me down a hallway to a back bedroom that served as her office. As we entered, I could smell the aroma of incense. She motioned me to a comfortable recliner chair as she sat at her desk chair, facing me.

"Well, it sounds like you've had a few trying weeks. Let's see if I can help you."

I told her briefly about the dream again and how it remained foremost in my mind. It seemed to be affecting me physically. I mentioned I had attended the dream class at the community college to find an answer. I even mentioned my dream book and analysis.

Ms. Tarver smiled. "You certainly have been diligent in your efforts, Jake." She hesitated for a second, then smiled. "Let's begin," she said.

She turned serious, and began. "With your background, I am first going to go over a few details that will give you an overview about my philosophy and methodology. Then I want to hear your dream."

She offered up a short prayer for my intentions. "Whenever I am uncertain about an issue, I ask for divine guidance," she explained.

Then she asked, "Jake, did you take the dream class at the junior college with Mrs. Evans?"

"Yes, I did."

"I want you to know that I really admire her. She is a great teacher and authority on dreams. However, she and I have fundamental differences. First, I have the belief that hypnosis can be used constructively in dream interpretation. I am a certified hypnotist. Mrs. Evans feels that hypnosis provides too much control and would yield unnatural responses. Secondly, I believe that it is very possible to contact a person who has already passed away and is in the spirit world. But don't worry. A person is naturally protected in this regard if he has a good relationship with his God. Mrs. Evans simply does not share that belief. These are two fundamental beliefs that Mrs. Evans and I do not share. Also, there is one more issue. I believe in reincarnation. More people than will admit to it do, too—I'd guess some eighty-five percent in the U.S., and closer to one hundred percent in Asian countries. Does … any of this bother you?"

"I've really not thought much about it. Basically, at this point I am really open to most anything. Are you—a psychic?"

"To be honest, I think I have a mild ability in this regard."

I nodded.

"Okay, Jake, do you remember from the conference what I said? If you don't understand your dreams don't worry, the Lord will make sure we understand just enough and that He Himself would take care of the rest. We'll do our best today, but don't fret. The answer eventually *will* come. Trust me, it will."

With this, she looked at me, and said, "Jake, take a deep breath."

I obliged and she resumed. "There are three kinds of dreams," she said. "There are psychological dreams, which have to do with the processing of what is currently on your mind. Next there are recreational dreams, which provide fun and enjoyment. Lastly, we have dreams with a spiritual theme that bear messages from our higher beings. We must remember that during our dreams our subconscious goes out to the universal stream of thought. Here it has unlimited potential. It can gather information, contact loved ones, travel and receive incredible messages. We each have an image of our highest source and we assign a face to that image. In essence, this is our God. If we are open, we can receive wonderful, transformational messages from our source. When you receive a significant message, you know that you did. Now this next point is extremely important, Jake. Some people have a hard time remembering their dreams because they are unable to confront the symbols that the subconscious mind provides them. This presents a problem."

She elaborated. "When I put a person under hypnosis, I utilize Gestalt principles. I believe a person is somehow intertwined to each and every aspect of his dream. Okay, Jake. Now I want you to tell me your dream."

I nodded, pulled out my typed sheet, and read:

"I am seated at a picnic table in a beautiful park-like setting on a sunny spring afternoon in the Midwest. Seated at my right is Carol, my high-school girlfriend from thirty-eight years ago. We are now married to other people. I ask her how many children she has. She answers three. I tell her that I have two. She looks at me, smiles, and then stands up. She says, 'Jake–would you attend a church retreat with me?' She turns to walk down a path toward the forest. Suddenly I see a man seated across from me. He is handsome with a dark complexion, dark hair, and neat goatee. He says, 'Carol is having some major problems and she really needs your help.' Somehow I had the feeling they were psychological issues. He continued, 'Will you help her?' Then I woke up."

For a long moment Ms. Tarver sat by silently. Then, "Jake, that is a very powerful dream," she said. "It is definitely spiritual in nature. When was the last time you talked to Carol?"

"It's been ... over thirty-eight years."

She thought for a moment. "May I ask you a personal question, Jake?"

"Sure," I replied.

"You're—happily married?"

"Absolutely."

She thought for a moment, "Well, I guess we can rule out a mid-life crisis," she smiled.

I laughed. "That is what my wife Julie made reference to."

Again she smiled.

"Did you attempt to call Carol?"

"No."

"I guess it would be kind of strange—I mean, after such a long period of time to call her unexpectedly and ask her if everything is okay. However, this really does sound like a call for help. Maybe she *is* in trouble, is calling or reaching out for your help. Let me tell you about a concept called 'shared dreams.' The events that happen in a dream with another person are in fact shared and remembered by the other person as well. This could be one possibility. She may also symbolize 'the younger Jake' from thirty-eight years ago or she may represent your feminine self. Or maybe she simply symbolizes youth and beautiful womanhood. Well, there'll be time for this later."

She shrugged. "So, Jake, let's move to the next process. We'll start out with a deep relaxation technique and attempt to get back into that dream.

First, close your eyes, relax, don't cross your feet or arms and try to get into a meditative position. I'm going to turn the light down. Please relax; I'm going to talk softly. This will help you to relax. I want you to relax your head, neck, shoulders, chest, stomach, arms, hands, legs, and feet. Take a deep breath. In one, two, three, and out one, two, three. When you exhale, imagine that your breath is letting all of your stress fall off you and onto the floor. Again with your next exhale, feel all the stress and tension just fall away. Relax now. Let waves of tension fall off your body onto the floor. Place your attention on your feet. Rotate your ankles, and relax. Point your toes, then relax them. Keep breathing in one, two, three, and out one, two, three. Relax any tightness in your feet. Just send your breath down to your feet and let your exhaled breath sweep away any tension that may be in your feet. Just let it go.

Going to the lower legs, the knees, and the legs. Release any tension you may have around your calves or knees. Tighten your thighs and relax. Now tighten your buttocks and relax. Really feel the sensation of staying on the chair and let go of all the muscles. Tighten your stomach and release. Feel the tension melt away. Breathe in one, two, three. Exhale one, two, three. Tighten your chest and relax. Tighten your forearms and biceps, then relax. Feel the tension leaving your body. Shrug your shoulders, then relax. Make a fist then relax. Let go of the tension in your arms and hands. Now, lift your eyebrows and relax. Squint, then relax. Pull the corners of your mouth back, then relax. Let go of all the tension in your body, Jake. Now breathe in one, two, three, and out one, two, three. Let all of your muscles go soft and relax. Feel yourself melting onto the chair. Release any tension. Just let yourself go. Just let it all go.

Let your breath go into your abdomen and sweep away any tension it may be holding and just let it go. Now let your exhale just sweep down your arms. Let your neck and shoulders go soft and relax. The muscles in the neck and shoulders—let them relax. Let go of all the tension in your neck and shoulders. Let any remaining tension slowly drift down your arms, and off your body. Let it fall to the floor. Continue to relax the muscles of your face. Let them relax. Release with your next breath, breathe and release. Now Jake, take a final check of your entire body.

It's a sunny beautiful afternoon and you're in a park. You see that there is a female with you. Look at the beautiful sky and what the trees look like. Sit down at the table and greet the female in the dream. Ask her if she has a message for you. Listen intently for her response. Now, as she makes her way down the path, acknowledge the male person in the dream— the man with the dark complexion and the goatee seated across from you. Ask him if he has brought the present—the box that contains the gift. Ask him to please hand you the box. There is something in the box. Now open the box and see what it contains. Reach into the box to receive your message, Jake. Then be silent. Thank them both for the gift and thank them for the wisdom they have shared.

I am now going to bring you back to the present. You are now walking away, back down the path following the woman. It's still a warm, beautiful sunny day. The sun feels warm to your skin as you're walking. With your next breath I want you to become more aware of the sounds around you. You're becoming more aware of the weight of your body sitting on a chair. You're almost ready to come back and now you can open your eyes.

Jake, tell me about the box."

I remember feeling like I was coming back from anesthesia. I replied, "It was a box about this size."

I described a box that was about a foot high, a foot wide, and a foot tall.

"The box was a silvery color with a very smooth, glossy finish. It reminded me of a beautiful Christmas gift box. The lid on the box came down over the sides significantly, by at least two inches. I opened the box and inside was a piece of paper that was folded."

Ms. Tarver exclaimed, "Ah, I knew it!"

"At first, I tried to open the paper, but I just couldn't. Finally, I believe that I was finally able to open the paper, but I couldn't see anything on the paper."

Ms. Tarver was smiling and chuckling. "You know why I'm laughing?" she asked. "Because, as soon as I told you to receive your message, I had an overwhelming thought that you were going to get a piece of paper. You asked me earlier if I was psychic. Well, I must be. At least a little bit."

"I couldn't see anything on the piece of paper," I added

"You couldn't read it?"

"Well, initially I thought I couldn't open it, but then I thought that it was a blank sheet of paper. I can't honestly tell you which one it was. Could this possibly mean that I'm not ready to receive the message?"

"That very well could be, Jake—good thought."

"Now about the woman—Carol—whom I talked to at the beginning. When I tried to talk to her, I got a feeling of peace and love and the colors blue and yellow. I was overwhelmed with a sense of happiness and joy, but I don't know what any of this means. I received more of a feeling from her rather than words or a sign."

"Well, in my experience, this dream is extremely important and spiritual in nature, Jake. Certainly you can repeat this analysis again on your own. You can also try to induce another dream to attempt to communicate with these people some more. Don't give up. You need to keep working on it."

I then asked, "What do you think? What does the paper represent? Do you have any thoughts?"

"Your initial analysis was right on. There was a message on the paper that you were obviously not yet ready to receive.

It's still hidden from you. It's funny, because I usually don't have insight into what a person is going to get, but for some odd reason I knew that you were going to get some piece of paper with something written on it. I didn't know if you'd be able to read it, because that would be pretty difficult your first time. However, you saw the message and that in itself is significant. You need to keep working at it. Now you have the technique and you can do this interpretive part. You can create your own 'relaxation tape,' if you want, to induce yourself into the deep relaxation. What I did with you was progressive relaxation. Progressive relaxation is pretty standard stuff.

After inducing a relaxed state, I typically suggest walking towards something. Sometimes I have people walking into a building, or a little wooden cabin, something like that. But since you already told me about the dream and it took place in the woods, I created the scenario of walking into a nature setting to help induce the dream. Then I suggest that you have the dialog with the people in your dream and receive a gift. I like to say they have a gift for you and to open the box because it gives the subconscious another opportunity to create a symbol, rather than just say speak to me or say something to me. Your subconscious likes to work in the language of symbols. It's easier that way, because that's how the mind works, in symbolic language. So when you ask for a gift in the box, the mind can handle that and create a symbol a lot easier than trying to come up with a dialogue. Sometimes one can achieve a dialogue, but it's easier to try to create a sign. That's the eyes-closed process. So now you have to continue to work the dream Jake. It will take some effort, but the answers will come."

"You mean, I have to figure out what this means on my own?" I inquired.

"Yes, you need to keep working using the same techniques. Try to induce another dream with the same characters. When you go to sleep at night say, 'I want to talk to Carol and the man in the dream. Tonight I'm going to have another dream about Carol and the dark complected man and this time I'm going to remember the dialogue I had with them. We'll be in a different place this time.' Or, 'I'm going to learn something from the dream, just a little something.' You know, don't make it too grandiose. You can induce a dream and ask to receive more information from these characters. I hope you now understand that it's not going to do you any good to get a book with a thousand and one dreams and look up, for example, the word 'paper.'"

"I did that," I replied." I now understand that the symbols can mean something to one person and something completely different to another. That's a waste of time."

"Yes, it is," continued Ms. Tarver. "I mean, there are symbols—archetypical symbols of water, for example— that mean death and rebirth, but then again it doesn't necessarily mean that at all. A church retreat is a place to receive knowledge. I believe this is what's happening in your dream. You were there to receive knowledge Jake. You told me that you thought the person was your shadow self, but this interpretation was not yours, but rather I assume it was suggested in your class as a potential interpretation. Don't get confused with dream books or philosophies. They're just going to baffle and bewilder you. When you said the man in your dream had a dark complexion and a goatee, it reminded me of someone, possibly from India. I thought, the man may be the cliché image of a spiritual teacher, a yogi. A yogi would be a person to provide you with some 'spiritual wisdom.' So Jake, if you continue to read dream symbol books that preserve traditional symbolism and they declare 'A dark character is evil or a shadow self and may depict your darkest fears,' that's going to mix you up."

"I'm ... trying to be open to everything," I interjected.

"Yes, and that's good," she replied. "But what you want to do is open yourself up to interact with the universal stream of consciousness when you're asleep," she added.

"So I've got to feel right about it," I said, "I need to choose what really feels right to me, on my own," I offered. "It is essentially up to me to interpret the symbols of my dream. I know I won't find the answers in a dream book."

"Yes, on *your* own Jake. The spiritual dream is one wherein you can communicate with your higher self or with a loved one who has passed over. As you become more adept at dreaming, you can tell which dreams are recreational dreams, and which dreams are deeply spiritual for you and very significant. You'll wake up sometimes and your mind will tell you as you are waking up, 'That dream was important. I'd better write that down. I know that was an important dream.' You will know that. Your own mind will tell you that. Other times you might have a dream about yourself as James Bond, which would be a more recreational dream. Your mind will go 'nah!' You will know in your heart and mind what's important."

"Is it possible that none of this interpretation means anything—that she is in fact in trouble?" I asked.

"It could be. When you're sleeping and open to that universal stream, you're available to receive messages from others. Yes, it could be. I'm not saying that it is for sure. On the one hand, it could mean that she represents the feminine side or your youthful self. But it could also mean that you're receiving a message from her and she in fact *is* reaching out."

Our session was over. Ms. Tarver once again repeated that with diligence the answer about my dream would be forthcoming. It would be up to me to continue the process. Yes, this was an important dream. I should not give up on it.

Chapter Five

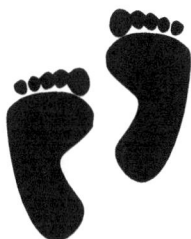

After the meeting, it was comforting to go home to Julie. As she prepared dinner, I set the table. We enjoyed a long, leisurely meal. We sat and talked for more than an hour. I gave her a play-by-play of the meeting and Julie really got a kick out of the fact that Ms. Tarver suggested the possibility that I was having a mid-life crisis.

Julie was fascinated but concerned that Ms. Tarver had hypnotized me to help me re-create and re-live my dream. Julie also shared and appreciated my frustration at not being able to read the paper from the box; to help me truly understand the intended message. I told her I needed to find a way to overcome my inability to continue the dream or to get the characters to meet with me in another dream as Ms. Tarver had suggested. I realized, as I shared with her, that I was ready for the task.

Each night I would start by praying. Then, as I started to doze off, I attempted to return to the dream. I would see Carol at the table and have the same conversation. It continued to be very difficult to have any further conversation with her. Each time I would attempt to engage her in a conversation, she would immediately start off towards the woods. So, I decided to focus on the yogi, to turn to him and attempt to pursue a conversation. However, each night when I attempted to engage Carol in conversation, my mind would quickly take me back to times I had with her thirty-eight years ago.

After a few of these unproductive nights, I remembered that Carol and I had parted on very strange terms, and I never really understood why. Without exception, the same pattern continued each and every night. As I attempted to engage Carol in conversation, I somehow grew mesmerized by her presence and was unable to take the next critical step.

So I decided to go directly to the yogi for the next few nights. But no. This did not work either. The yogi would not appear. It seemed that I had no choice. I needed to go through Carol to get the initial process going. But, as night after night would prove, I could never progress from that point. I even tried to induce another dream with the hopes of meeting the characters. Again, to no avail.

After about ten days of little sleep and continued headaches, it grew apparent that something had to break soon, if only to preserve my sanity. The thoughts of the dream lingered. Ever since my initial dream, I realized that the only success I had was due to Ms. Tarver's hypnosis. It was now readily apparent that I could not do this by myself. But Julie did not want me to go the hypnosis route again. She was very apprehensive about it and vehemently shared her concerns. We both, however, felt strongly that the message was extremely important. So where did that leave me? Was I denying some aspect of my subconscious 'shadow self' and hurting my ability to make contact? Maybe I was just not ready for the message or, was Carol *really* calling out to me?

That next night I prayed and tried not to think about the dream. As I lay in bed a thought came. I remembered Ms. Tarver's words. "If you don't understand your dreams, don't worry. The Lord will make sure we understand just enough, and He Himself will take care of the rest." Maybe I should do a little more praying and less worrying.

I had the dream again that night, but this time, I woke with a thought. The only thing I really had not truly considered was that Carol was in desperate need of help. Sure, I had tried to get the message without sticking my neck out, but if I really wanted to find that answer, it would require a telephone call.

Through years of habit I had religiously included Carol when I prayed for others' intentions. I guess at one time I was so used to being with her that I never broke the pattern. I had once heard that if a person really wanted to help another, simply praying for the intentions of that person would be enough to put you in mental contact with that person. Praying for them would then assist in limiting this person's troubles or issues.

Was the dream prompting me to make a call? The dream class had taught me to take some chances and to go with my gut feeling. Would it validate my belief in dreams?

I thought long and hard. Just what would a person do for a friend? Would he be willing to look foolish with a slim chance of aiding the other at her time of need—if, in fact, there were an actual need? After all, it had been thirty-eight years. Simply, it would sound far too bizarre. Julie supported me either way, but the decision she told me was solely mine.

In the end I felt that I owed it to Carol to take the chance.

It was the Christian thing to do. In the nearly three years we went together, I had been extremely fortunate. She was an incredible person of faith. That night, March 23, I got home and decided to call. It was time to find the answer. *Was* she in fact calling out to me? I knew that she lived in Iowa, and an on-line search quickly retrieved her telephone number. I sat silently in my office for about an hour. Finally, with a burst of courage, I punched the numbers. As the phone rang four times, I got too nervous and hung up. It reminded me of when I had first called her on the phone my junior year of high school to ask for her help on a history assignment that I had actually already completed.

After about five minutes I felt a new surge of energy, and again made the call. This time I did hang on. After about six rings, a recording kicked in: "Hi, this is the Sanders residence. We are not available right now, so please leave a message at the tone and we will call you back as soon as we can."

Stunned to hear her voice after almost forty years, I tried to put my thoughts together quickly, and managed a cryptic message.

"Hi, Carol. If you need anything at all, call me at 480-408-4224. Wherefore art thou? This—is Jake."

I hung up, to an immense feeling of relief. After only seconds, however, the relief shifted into disappointment. I felt like an idiot. I rehashed what I had said. Couldn't I have been clearer, smarter? Would she recall the quote from Shakespeare? We had spent a great deal of time on this play our senior year in high school.

For the next few weeks, the dream continued—as images during the day and in full color each night. Somehow, though, the headaches had vanished. But I was still getting little sleep. Despite all of this, I settled back into my normal routine at work, and it seemed that the dream was less in our conversations at home. As days turned into weeks, I started to feel embarrassed. Why had I made the call? Although I felt the dream still had some merit, I was beginning to think that maybe I had been the victim of some mind game. What was I thinking? However, when I started to think this way I got a gut feeling that somehow with patience and time, there would be an answer. But up to this point the only legitimate analysis had come via the two dream professionals. Each had thought a message would soon be at hand. Each, it now seemed, was mistaken.

It was on a Monday evening exactly two weeks after I had called Carol that our phone rang. I remember looking at the clock. It was 7:19 p.m. Julie answered. With an odd look on her face, she announced, "Honey, it's for you." She handed the phone to me. "It's Carol!"

A chill gripped my body. I stood up, edged over, took the phone, stepped limply into my office. I offered a hello.

I heard the familiar voice; its inflexion so familiar. Against my heart-thumps, Carol spoke calmly. "Jake, thanks for calling. I was really surprised to hear from you. I really appreciate your concern. Apparently—how, I don't know—you must have heard. Yes, my husband Jim suffered a heart attack about six weeks ago. He died very quickly. And, yes, I'm in a fog trying to cope. We were all trying to cope—to make arrangements, you know—otherwise I would have called you much sooner."

"Carol? I am so sorry to hear about Jim. You have my deepest sympathy."

No, I wouldn't tell her. Suddenly that I had called her simply because of a dream made no sense at all. We talked for another five minutes, until her daughter interrupted.

"Jake, I need to go. But if you ever get in the area, please stop in. I'd love to see you again. Thank you for remembering me. And, oh, by the way—'Wherefore art thou?'"

We each said goodbye, and hung up.

Still in a daze, I told Julie about the conversation. We both were shocked to hear that something so traumatic had happened to her. Julie and I both said a prayer for Carol's intensions.

Then I asked Julie, "Do you think the dream was a signal to me?"

"Absolutely, without any question," she replied.

Somehow, we figured, I had received a signal that Carol was in trouble and had sensed her pain. Immediately I thought that this dream analysis had its purpose. There actually was something to it. But with all I had learned during the last month, it just didn't feel right that my message would end with this discovery. It didn't seem that the underlying reason for the dream would be to call Carol to pay my condolences.

Julie ran out and got a sympathy card. We would put it

in the mail tomorrow. That night we went to bed early. As usual, I prayed for everyone's intentions, including Carol's. Again the dream hung foremost in my mind. Again it played out the same way, now with even more thoughts of Carol and myself years before. With all that had transpired with Carol and the dream, I had not told Julie about these details in the new dreams. I was sure they meant nothing. I knew I loved my wife dearly and I would never want to hurt her.

At work the next day, I learned that Ben had been called for jury duty. He had always boasted that he could find a way out of it, but this time he was mistaken. What's more, the case he was chosen for was estimated to last for at least two weeks. Our firm's president, Lou Walters, was scrambling to find someone to replace Ben at a few critical meetings over the next ten days. He mentioned it at our weekly staff meeting, and asked for a volunteer. The trip would involve meetings with two potential clients and would require a flight to Dubuque and then on to Milwaukee.

As I got back to my office, it hit me. Carol was in Iowa. I got a map out. Lo and behold, she lived between Dubuque and Milwaukee. I called Julie, asked her about the trip.

"Honey, I believe that this happened for a reason," she said. "I trust you and love you. Maybe you should go and provide her with some support. I know how caring you are. You know the right thing to say at the right time. Remember how you helped me when Dad died? You have a real gift."

"Wow," I answered. I had forgot about that time in our lives. "Julie—thanks."

I went in to see Mr. Walters. He was pleased that I volunteered for the assignment, especially on such short notice. When I asked him for an extra day or two to aid an old friend, he nodded.

"That will not be a problem, Jake. Remember we not only help companies–we help people."

He looked me up and down. "Jake, I've always admired you. You are a very kind, family man with great financial talent. In many ways you are a perfect example of our company mission statement. I ... thank you for that."

I called our administrative secretary to make the arrangements. She secured rooms in Dubuque and Milwaukee with no problem. In helping me make my McGregor reservations she had run into a problem. Most of the hotels in the immediate area were booked, but she did secure me a room at a local bed and breakfast. I would be leaving in a few days.

That night I told Julie about the arrangements. She suggested I call Carol right away. I obliged. This time I was less apprehensive. Carol was excited and looking forward to the visit. I told her my time frame, and she gave me directions to her town and house. That night I said special intentions for everyone and prayed that the trip would be a positive experience for all. And once again, I dreamed of Carol at the park.

Monday morning came. My flight was at 7 a.m. Julie dropped me off at six. The flight would make a quick stopover in Minneapolis, then depart for Dubuque. Julie gave me a big kiss, a long hug. "Honey, I love you. Be safe and be careful. Now—go do your magic. The Lord be with you."

With that I told her again that I loved her, and edged out.

Chapter Six

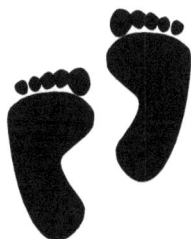

The plane was not crowded. I was fortunate to have a three-seat section in the front of the plane all to myself. I could get some work done on the way, I thought. With a slight chill in the cabin, the flight attendant offered me a blanket. I guess the combination of the cool air, the blanket, and the motion was what put me to sleep.

Once again I dreamed of Carol at the park. This time the dream took me back to the summer of 1966. It was the first time I had ever seen her. Our local legion post was having a summer's-end dance for high-school students on the last Saturday night of the summer. The dance ended up more as a concert, as not too many people—including myself—were willing to dance. We just sat around in groups and chatted. I remember hearing the Doors' song "Light My Fire." I always loved that song. The Doors recorded both long and short versions of the song. I relished both.

It was during that song that I spotted Carol. Even thought I didn't yet know her, that song soon would became synonymous with her. She was standing with a group of girls laughing and talking. Her lovely face, unusually light blond hair, and slender body reminded me of a princess. A friend said that her name was Carol, that she had just moved to town. Her beauty mesmerized me. She immediately became popular at school. Before long she had been voted student-council president. As school started, I remember attending a donkey basketball game at school where the teachers took on the student council. She was one of the few to score a basket.

It took me more than a year to finally meet her. I remember sitting in chemistry class one morning in September of 1967. A girlfriend of hers told me there was someone who "really liked" me. She told me that her name was Carol. She said that the someone was the cute blonde girl who is our student-council president. I told her that I didn't believe her, but I recall entertaining a slight ray of hope. Later that day the same friend reappeared in the hallway. "Jake—come over here," she said. I walked over. There stood Carol, with a broad smile. "Hi," I said, and then quickly found a way to excuse myself. I remember feeling awkward, not knowing what to say. I simply lacked confidence—especially with this "total ten." Later that same day, Carol came and sat beside me in study hall. I remember making some dumb jokes, and recalled that her laugh was infectious. I convinced myself she was only being kind. I *was* quarterback on the football team, and extremely confident on the field, but in this situation, I was ever so shy. Yet she made it easy for me because she was so friendly and always smiling. I liked her from the start. She was beautiful. Honesty, innocence, naiveté—these were her finest qualities.

After a few weeks, I finally got the courage to ask her if she would like to go golfing with my brother Mike and me on a Saturday morning. She attended the Friday-night football game the night before, and I remember looking over and seeing her in the crowd. She smiled at me when I ran out onto the field. Saturday morning, Mike and I drove to her house to pick her up for golf. I had thought it would be much easier if I had a little buffer, some help on my first date, so I enlisted Mike.

It was a beautiful, sunny day. When we arrived at Carol's house, I was amazed to find that she lived in a part of town dense with trees. Her home had recently been built, tucked away from view on the street. As we drove down her long driveway, it felt like I was entering a lush forest. I remarked to Carol about the beautiful trees. She told me her family loved and appreciated being surrounded by nature's beauty. We had a very enjoyable time that day. I learned it was her first time golfing, and found her golf skill to be mediocre. However, what I remember most was her willingness to try and to laugh at her own mistakes. It didn't take me long to ask her out on another date–for the following Friday night after our afternoon football game. We attended a movie at the local theater. I wanted to hold her hand so badly, but I didn't know how she would react. At the end of the evening, I walked her to her door. I prayed for courage, but couldn't gather enough nerve to kiss her. At the door, I extended my arm and then shook her hand.

The next week we attended a school dance on Saturday night. When I took her home, I asked her if she wanted to talk. She agreed. We sat in the car in her secluded driveway until 1:30 a.m., chatting straight through. I had no idea we had been in the car so long. That night I fell in love with her hook, line, and sinker. At her door, I found my courage. I leaned over and kissed her good night. I saw stars! I was in seventh heaven the entire drive home. I didn't even remember driving, all I could think about was Carol and the wonderful time we had chatting and getting to know each other. It was the best night of my life. I was left floating on cloud nine.

I got home at two—a full two hours past my curfew. My Mom was furious and grounded me for two weeks. I remember thinking the grounding had been worth it, every minute. After what seemed to be a very long two weeks, Carol and I started dating again.

Over the next few weeks, I learned more and more about her. She was a very talented dancer, specializing in 'tap dance,' thanks to years of lessons and practice. Her favorite outfit was a navy-blue sailor suit. Blue was such a great color on her, and brought out the sparkle in her eyes. Her little finger had a slight bend in it. I told her it was a good thing. I would never get her mixed up with anyone else. My comment made her laugh. Finally, the more I interacted with her family, I realized that she was the loving product of a very kind, wonderful family.

The Sadie Hawkins Day dance was looming. I felt honored when she asked me to be her date. We went on a hayride, dressed as farmers. She even had freckles painted on her face.

Carol and I were now a couple and "going together." We seemed inseparable. Little by little, shyness was leaving me. She had given me newfound confidence. I became more outgoing and made new friends. My new friends shared that my shyness had been misinterpreted as being aloof and conceited. Carol helped me to reach out and connect with others. To have friends, you must be a friend. Carol helped me overcome my shyness, which I came to learn was a barrier to making friends. Often the shy don't believe people will like them just the way they are—which is why they're standoffish to begin with. A no-win situation!

We continued to date each weekend, usually ending the night with lengthy talks at the end of her driveway. Here we felt secure, as if we were in our own little world. We enjoyed the seclusion and tranquility and Carol referred to it as "our little piece of heaven." Her parents knew our schedule and would signal us on many a night with a flick of the outside lights, to remind us it was time to end our evening. When we were together, we oftentimes lost track of time. Time passed so quickly when we were together. Sometimes on Saturday nights we ended up in her family room. We would watch professional football highlights and she would make what I considered the "world's greatest hamburger."

It was a wonderful fall season. We attended homecoming together and were both members of the homecoming court. This made the weekend festivities even more special for us. We enjoyed every unique moment from the bonfire, the game, dinner, and finally the homecoming dance. A few weeks later, I took Carol to a burger joint in the nearby town. She ordered a "Black Cow," a chocolate drink. This was an unusual choice for Carol, since she usually preferred drinks with fruit such as raspberries and strawberries. The chocolate drink didn't agree with her. I had to rush her home and I remember it being the shortest date we ever had.

We enjoyed being together and laughed at everything. The slightest thing would start a wave of hysterical laughter, sometimes for hours at a time. She liked my constant puns. However, on rare occasions she would remark, "Jake, that joke stunk, and was only two thirds of a pun–PU!"

Winter came. I was on the basketball team, and she attended all the games. Like me, she absolutely loved basketball. She understood the meaning of the game–its beauty and teamwork. We both loved the smell of popcorn when we walked into the gym. During games she would usually sit with my family.

These had been great times. Basketball was my favorite sport, and I was thrilled to find someone who loved it as well. She attended all the games, home and away, and waited for me after each game. As we talked for hours, she would give me insight into her thoughts on the game. I would listen to her commentary and sometimes kid her about her analysis. She really did have a good understanding of the game. What a wonderful friend and sounding board! She knew how much I loved the Supremes and would listen to them before every game for good luck. She bought me their album. She loved the Carpenters and would sing their songs. We loved the Association. "Cherish" was our signature song; it would forever bind us and be special.

One Saturday night we attended a movie. I had warned her that it might be a bit scary, but she was willing to go, of course. The movie, *Wait Until Dark*, featured Audrey Hepburn as a young woman who had recently become blind.

Unknown to her, her photographer husband brought home a doll he was holding as a favor for a woman he had met on an international flight. The doll contained heroin. A gang of smugglers posing as police officers were able to gain her confidence and enter the apartment to find the doll. The young woman hastily removed every light bulb in the apartment in an attempt to even the playing field. However, she forgot one–the refrigerator light. At one point in the movie, all the lights were turned off in the theater. Then, set in the kitchen, came the climax of the movie—the villain lunging with a knife at the poor woman out of the darkness, aided by the lone refrigerator light. The audience screamed. I physically jumped myself. I had never heard Carol scream before and really didn't like it.

As I drove Carol home, I couldn't help but notice that she still appeared to be visibly shaken from the movie. She sat very close to me, which to me, was a good thing. I apologized for the movie choice, but she generously indicated there was no need to apologize. When we finally reached Carol's driveway, we couldn't help but notice that all the lights in her house were off. As we stared at the dark house, we spotted a tiny light moving from room to room. Carol was frantic about her family's safety and began to cry. I quickly backed out and drove to the local police department a few miles down the road and explained the circumstances. We followed the police back to her home. An officer approached the front door, and rang the doorbell. Carol's Dad appeared, a candle in hand. He explained to the police officer that the electricity had gone out and he was checking the breakers to attempt to restore the power. Carol was relieved, but I was quite embarrassed.

Spring brought prom, another special time. We double-dated with my close friend Dan and his girlfriend Ann. Again we were fortunate, Carol and I had been honored to represent our class on prom court. We enjoyed a wonderful dinner, dance, and post-prom. In the wee hours of the morning, we decided it was time to end the wonderful night. Since early evening, it had been pouring rain and Ann lived on a farm. As we carefully pulled into her driveway, Dan's car got stuck in a large rut in the mud. We were wedged in the mud for more than an hour. Dan, a slightly built guy, asked Ann if she wouldn't mind getting out of the car and pushing in the downpour. After all, wasn't she much bigger and stronger than he? "It just makes more sense," he said. Never in my life did I see Carol laugh so hard. Her laughter was uncontrollable. Finally the rain eased, and Dan and I rocked and pushed the car, while Carol drove our way to freedom. To this day, I think, Ann is still miffed at Dan.

As summer approached, we would go for long rides through the rolling hills of southern Wisconsin. One of our favorite spots was an observation tower six stories high located in a forested state park. If you climbed to the top on a clear day, it was said that you could see twenty-six different lakes. We notched our initials at the top of the tower as a sign of our love. We made numerous trips to the Dog and Suds, as we both loved ice cream. We would drive to the local lake and walk through the woods to the beach. I would always hold her hand, ensuring that she would never trip on the rugged pathway. We spent more hours together in her driveway talking about life. These talks are probably what I remember and cherish the most about her. Evening after evening Carol would rebound for me as I practiced my jump shot at her house in the hope of landing a basketball scholarship to college. She herself had a very nice shot. It was a shame that women didn't have the same opportunities as men at that time. Thank God for Title Nine!

After Carol spent a weekend in Chicago with my family at my cousin's house, she invited me to spend a weekend with her family at their cabin in northern Wisconsin. Her family had gone to the lake for three weeks every summer. I'll never forget the weeks she was gone. I missed her so much. I remember driving for hours to meet them, listening to "White Rabbit" by the Jefferson Airplane along the way. I was so excited to finally get to see her. She had set her hair all day in honor of my arrival and she looked as beautiful as ever. Moments later, we walked to the end of the pier and— she slipped and fell in the lake. I jumped in and retrieved her, but I still remember how bad she felt about her hair. It was however, a wonderful three days, including several fish dinners and a memorable night at a drive-in. I think we must have heard "Cherish" four times that evening alone.

The 4th of July was always a fun time in our small town. Together, we attended our town's annual Fourth of July parade. It lasted for a few hours and was always entertaining.

Carol especially liked the clowns.

As time went by we seemed inseparable. I could count on her. She could count on me. No matter what, I could always make her laugh. Sticking straws in my nose or ears or talking in some made-up language seemed to do the trick. By our senior year we knew each other's family very well. We were both Lutheran, a great fit. We even attended church together, most weeks.

I remember working construction the summer before my senior year. One day we labored at a site near Carol's house. She asked me to come over for lunch that day. I remember looking at her in a different light. I think we both felt it. It was like we were married and I was coming home for lunch. After that day, we talked about marriage. She wanted to have six kids. I wanted four. I gave her my class ring as a token of my love and promised I would replace it with a permanent one as soon as I could.

We were fated to be together forever. With all the football, basketball, dances, parties, and once again homecoming and prom, our senior year flew by. I had a car that year, and was able to take her to school each day. We both enjoyed seeing each other every day. I enjoyed seeing the sun light up and dance across her face each morning as we turned on to the main road away from the woods. Every afternoon, she would wait for me after practice and I would take her home. During practice she would take the car to run errands with her friends. How cool, I thought, that she was using my car! I remember being invited to dinner on many occasions. Fish, especially smelt, seemed to be a family favorite. Carol's dad loved to fish. Fish meals were plentiful and oftentimes shared with me. One Saturday night in the late fall, the dinner went very late and since I was extremely tired, Carol invited me to stay overnight. I slept in their spare bedroom upstairs. It seemed so odd to see her first thing in the morning, but in a way almost felt like a preview of our future. For Christmas I wanted to get her something special. I spied a huge, five-foot-tall stuffed dog in a store window one day. My mom agreed to pay half the cost, but reminded me that I would have to earn my portion. I got a job, and true to my word, earned my half. Early on Christmas Eve morning, my Mom spent at least two hours wrapping the dog in a huge box. I remember feeling proud to give her something so special. Carol was shocked to see the huge box! She loved her 'new dog.'

Easter was equally special for us. Carol and I attended church with our families. Afterwards, we returned to my house to find the Easter baskets my mom painstakingly hid for every member of the family and Carol as well. I was amused, as I watched her search for her basket and noticed the relief on her face when she found hers before I found mine. We saw *The Graduate* together. I told her that if she were ever in that position, I would do the same thing at the church. Nothing would keep us apart. Watching *Hawaii Five-O* was another favorite family pastime. Carol would oftentimes come over and watch with my family. The famous line—"Book 'em, Danno," was our favorite. Another movie we saw together and enjoyed was *Butch Cassidy and the Sundance Kid*. I felt so lucky to have a girlfriend who enjoyed and appreciated Westerns. But of all the movies, I think be both enjoyed the mystique of the James Bond genre. When we were together, she made me feel like 007. Indeed, we had shared so many wonderful memories together—and this would be just the *beginning*.

In the spring of 1969, I made several recruiting trips to a variety of colleges for basketball. Carol came with me on one of the trips. We got up early and made the three-hour drive. On the way we stopped at a park and took in its beauty. When we arrived at the school, I introduced Carol to the coach. I remember him being thoroughly impressed. We had lunch together, and later in the day I got a chance to play with the returning team members. Carol watched the practice and I remember playing very well. We returned home positive and happy. We had spent the entire day together. On the way home, I asked her, "What does this remind you of?"

"Like being married," she replied.

"Me, too," I told her.

Of all our times together, senior English class will always stand out. To me it was by far our finest hour. Our class studied Shakespeare, and we were fortunate to be in the same class. We had finished *Hamlet* and started to study *Romeo and Juliet*. At the time I did not realize the lasting effect this play would have on our lives.

One day our teacher seemed upset as he spoke to the class. Many students were relying on Cliff Notes instead of reading the actual play. In an effort to curb this behavior, he told the class that the Cliff Notes would not work with *Romeo and Juliet*. In fact, if we didn't read the play carefully, we would suffer the consequences on the test. Carol and I had aced the previous tests and intended to do the same on the upcoming test. It being Friday, we had only three days until the test and we had yet read the play. We agreed to work, no matter how long it took to read and analyze the entire play. We spent Friday night, all day Saturday and Sunday together. We never worked so hard. We read the entire play—each and every line. We took scenes apart, analyzed elements. We knew all the details and understood all of the symbolism. From start to finish we felt its pulse. From Romeo's first confession of his love from a distance to its confirmation shortly after, we felt the essence. We even duplicated their first kiss several times. I kept telling her that I didn't think we really had it down pat! We understood the magnitude of this kiss, especially when they yet did not know each other's names. We were saddened by Juliet's predicament, her father's wishes for her and Paris. We read and reread Juliet's most famous line— "O Romeo, Romeo! Wherefore art thou, Romeo. Deny thy father and refuse thy name; Or, if thou wilt not, be but sworn my love, And I'll no longer be a Capulet." We sensed her frustration. We felt her predicament and agreed she should marry for love and not because of someone else's agenda. We were saddened by the feud between the Capulets and the Montagues and the lives sacrificed as a result. We nervously read on as Juliet drank the potion in hopes she would appear dead. We were devastated when the message of her plan never reached Romeo. Our hearts were saddened when Romeo took his own life and we cried when Juliet awoke to find him dead. We suffered more as Juliet kissed his poisoned lips to no avail. As we read with tears in our eyes, Juliet pushed his dagger into her chest, then fell, lifeless, atop his body. It just didn't seem fair to us that they would never have their earthy love due to circumstances they *couldn't* control.

The dye was cast. It was difficult for us to accept that the lovers never got the chance to say *goodbye* to each other. We promised that would *never* happen to us. Fate had dealt them a bad hand. For over two days we danced, laughed, cried, lived—acted the parts and loved. We felt the desires, passion, and pain of these star-crossed lovers. We became one with the play. It was a fairy tale weekend, one never to forget.

By late Sunday night we felt a special bond with each other and with a special play that I, will always remember. We were Romeo and Juliet. The bond had somehow raised our relationship to a new level—ironically, all in the name of schoolwork!

Carol ended up getting 100% on the test. I received a 99.

I suddenly felt a slight tug on my shoulder. The flight attendant notified me that we had arrived in Minneapolis. Apparently, I had slept the entire flight. And now I was starting to remember my dream. Had someone … sprinkled a potion on me? So it seemed. A potion that would allow me to recall so many of the details from those bygone times, details I had not thought of for years.

It was as if someone had turned on a faucet and moments from my past had come rushing out.

Chapter Seven

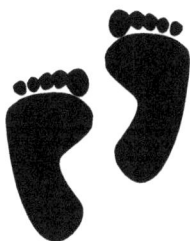

In thirty minutes we would depart for Dubuque. I remained in the same seat, thinking of the dream and its remarkable details. Just before takeoff I was joined by a late arrival, a woman who, by the logo on her briefcase, worked for another prominent insurance company. I introduced myself and told her I also worked in the insurance industry. She told me her name, Cindy, and added that she was on her way to a regional meeting. As the flight took off, I again started to doze. Soon I was asleep. Again the dream— Carol in the park. My thoughts now went to late in our senior year. With graduation approaching, we were both concerned about the upcoming year. We had much to be thankful for. I'll never forget holding her on graduation night–neither one of us wanted to say goodnight. We agreed that someday soon we would never have to say goodnight again. We made a promise to stay together.

We both worked full time over the summer, which made the days go by quickly. But, just like the song "The Summer of 69," these *were* "the best days of our lives." We attended parties, went to the beach, had little responsibility outside of our jobs, and saw each other each night. At summer's end Dan married Ann. I was his best man.

It was a beautiful service in a quaint little church. Excitement filled the air. When the two began to say their vows, I peeked back momentarily to Carol. We smiled at each other. Someday we, too, would repeat these same precious words when our special time came. A few weeks later, one of Carol's friends from work got married, and we drove to the wedding. As Carol turned to get out of the car, the back seam of the zipper on her dress simply unraveled, exposing her back. Since it was a very hot July day, Carol had not brought along a shawl. I took my sport coat off and draped it over her. Only a moment before the ceremony, we filed into the back of church and edged into a pew. There she sat, the entire wedding, with my coat over her. When someone asked, I told them she wasn't feeling well, that she was a bit cold.

Autumn came. I had received a full basketball scholarship, and went off to college to play hoops. Carol was accepted at the same school. It took enormous pressure off me when I found out that we would both attend the same college. We would not have the added pressure of a long distance relationship. I had worried for a long time, but didn't mention my concern to Carol. We could now be together *all* the time.

The first week at school was sheer fantasy. However, our freedom and time together was short lived. That weekend she told me her family was having major financial difficulty. Her dad told her they were unable to come up with the money to pay her tuition. Sadly, she had no choice. She was forced to leave. With a heavy heart, she gathered up all her things from her room, and headed home, to attend the local junior college.

I remember being devastated and hoped this would not strain our relationship. We had never planned on being apart from each other. It bothered me far more than I ever shared with her. With time, I realized that we have to learn to accept some things and move on. It was a difficult transition, but I felt we could survive. After all, aren't plants often divided to insure proper growth? We, too, could grow and, in the end, find a healthier, happier life together.

I knew in my heart that she wanted to marry soon. I wanted to marry Carol, but I had seen couples who wed too early and sacrifice their futures. It seemed best to wait. In time, we could have it all. It seemed very logical to me.

Carol attended some of my games, but distance became a factor. As a result, we didn't see each other as much. Then summer came. I had a job on a local golf course as a greens-keeper, working long hours seven days a week. It left little time for Carol. One of my jobs was to turn the water on nightly for each of the nine greens. I would drive my dad's car from one green to the next and turn the water on. An hour later I would repeat the drive, turning the water off. Many times Carol would accompany me, my only chance to see her that day. I remember kissing her on every green each night for good luck. How lucky was I to have such a supportive friend and girlfriend!

We didn't spend as much time together that summer that we had both anticipated after the long school year. By the end of the summer Carol seemed somewhat aloof. I remember thinking that it had been a tough few months, but we both knew that someday soon we would be together. We parted again as I headed back to school. Unknown to me at the time, I was about to begin one of the toughest times of my entire life. Academics were difficult the first semester of my sophomore year and basketball incredibly demanding. The university had moved up from Division II to Division I, which added significantly to the pressure. We started practicing early in the fall with weights, runs, and open-gym games. Many national recruits had been signed to compete on this level. Many solid players from our local area—standouts in their own right—were quickly cut. Fortunately, I survived the onslaught. I was determined to make it for us. As the season progressed, I started to consistently have pain in my knee. I tried to ignore the symptoms and continued to play.

I didn't own a car, and Carol didn't attend any of my games. However, one night I thought I saw her. We were warming up for a home game against Long Beach State. I had just taken a lay-up and was jogging to the rebounding line when I noticed a familiar shock of blonde hair moving through the crowd. The hair was so distinctive. It had to be Carol. Immediately, I felt a surge of excitement. For the next few minutes, adrenalin pumped through my body. My heart beat faster. I tried to get a better look in her direction but at the same time was forced to concentrate on basketball. A short time later, the girl came down the bleachers and walked right past me. As she came closer, my excitement turned to disappointment. It wasn't Carol.

Up to that point I had convinced myself that it really was her. How I missed her! I remember thinking that we were beginning to drift apart. She probably didn't know that I thought about her and prayed for her every day. More than anything I wanted to marry her, but I had not even declared a major yet, and I really loved playing basketball. Now would not be the time. I was a young man trying to get his bearings straight. I simply had nothing to offer her, at least not yet. I intended to wait and make the fairytale come alive. I would be the knight in shining armor, and show up on a white horse with my college diploma in hand and kneel in her presence. Happily, I would pop the magical question, with a sparkling diamond ring in hand. Then, two soul-mates would be bonded in time.

Within a month Carol left a message for me to call her. I did, and she said that she wanted to see me. I was so excited that she would make the trip all the way just for me. I remember cleaning the apartment and then biding time for over an hour, nervously anticipating her arrival. She finally arrived. When she entered the apartment I gave her a big hug and kiss, but she pulled back, sullen. Then suddenly she meekly announced, "Jake—I came to say goodbye," but she would not look me in the eye. I was absolutely stunned, dazed, and could not think straight. I told her I loved her, but she looked away and said she had to go. She didn't want to talk about it. The meeting I so looked forward to lasted only three minutes. I had planned to take her down to the lake to talk, but I never even got a chance.

Without a car and very little money, I still tried to contact her. I borrowed money and sent her flowers. I borrowed a friend's car and drove to her work—only to have her walk away from me. I wrote her letters, many letters. It seemed that my communications were not being delivered or were somehow lost in translation. Just what *if* our love was now lost because we could not find words to say to one another? I took a small loan, bought an engagement ring, drove with a friend out to the park near her house. Carol and I had often visited this park for picnics. I sat at our picnic table, waited as my friend drove to Carol's. It seemed that this would be my final hope. I peered at the ring several times, hoping that, true to its form, it would be well received. It was the longest half-hour of my life.

When my friend arrived at Carol's home he told her, "Jake needs to talk to you desperately. Would you please come to the park, Carol?" But my friend returned to the park that afternoon alone.

As he walked up, my heart sank. "Jake, I'm really sorry. She said she just couldn't come."

I was beside myself. Was this fate knocking at my door? What would have been the result of our meeting? I would never know. It really bothered me that we didn't even part as friends. I found myself bewildered and confused. Why couldn't she face me? I ran many scenarios through my mind. Did she have a new boyfriend? What were her plans? I knew she wanted to get married, and now my own education and basketball seemed like selfish desires. Had they contributed to the downward spiral of our relationship?

I had convinced myself that I was getting my degree for her, not in spite of her. However, now I felt selfish. We had lost our ability to communicate, so the truth became lost in the process. My priorities were no longer her priorities.

We had moved from a private, trusting relationship to one susceptible to outside factors. I had gotten lost, and somehow she didn't bother to find me. Just as with Romeo and Juliet, a force was in play–a disruptive force that overcame our bond. We were apart due to each of our individual needs. Our separation had led to choices that dulled our passion for each another.

Was there a poison? Could outside rumors with enough force to tempt even the strongest of believers lead to the destruction of our relationship? Did taking the longer, winding road to finish college and play basketball before marrying and spending eternity together turn out to be our downfall? There were no immediate answers. Just like Romeo and Juliet, there was no true villain.

We were just two good people who had tasted the poison of the real world.

Basketball continued. I seemed to play on autopilot. It was difficult but nonetheless, I went through the motions. Fortunately, I loved basketball and felt a strong sense of responsibility to the school. Near the end of the season my knee really started bothering me again. This time, however, I sought medical attention. My knee required surgery and a week of hospitalization. By then it was spring break, so I returned home to recuperate with a full-length cast on my leg.

One day, glancing through the local paper, I spotted Carol's wedding announcement. I was absolutely crushed. In just a few days Carol would be married in our church. I can't deny that I considered the church scene from *The Graduate*, but logic soon returned. I knew I had to respect her choice, her privacy. I remember praying for her intentions that day, just as I had every day since we had met. I had to love her enough to let her go. This was very difficult. I hoped she had found true happiness. The wedding hour came, then went. I knew she now belonged to someone else. I felt such an overwhelming sense of loss. That day, I lost not only the love of my life, but my best friend. My Juliet was gone forever.

Several weeks later I got rid of my cast. However, even after extensive rehabilitation, my knee just wasn't the same. The injury and subsequent surgery hampered my ability to cut properly and jump off my left leg. My basketball ability would never be what it was.

Within a few months, I had lost the two things I had loved the most. What saddened me the greatest, was that I never got a chance to say goodbye to Carol—to say goodbye on my terms. I never had the opportunity to tell her what was in my heart. As we had previously learned studying *Romeo and Juliet*, I felt the reality and sadness that not saying goodbye left. This bothered me more than anything.

"Are you okay?"

I was startled and woke on my own, in a flutter.

"Fine—just a slight nightmare," I managed. Cindy just smiled.

I sensed a pain deep in my stomach, a pain I had not felt for a long, long time but one with a familiar, far-reaching sting. Was this the demon that was ruling my dream? Was this my shadow self? Was this symbolic of the quest I was on? Right then, an unusual memory came to mind from Romeo and Juliet. In Mercutio's Act Four speech he refers to the "Fairy Queen Mab," who delivers dreams to dreamers. I remembered that Mab's dreams were thought not to bring out our positive aspects but rather to isolate and illustrate our poorer qualities. Was this more evidence that I had a score to settle with my Shadow Self? Was my subconscious about to surface?

We made our decent into Dubuque. Soon I had my luggage and was on my way in a rental car. The Iowa landscape looked different. The air felt cool. By mid-afternoon on a slightly overcast day, I found my motel and settled in without difficulty. I had a wonderful plate of lasagna at a local Italian restaurant, then went for a short walk. Back in my room I called Julie and reported that I was fine. The rest of the evening I spent preparing for the next day's meeting with our new client. I also called Carol and told her my schedule. After the meetings, I planned to drive to McGregor, where I had reserved three nights lodging. She gave me directions and told me to call if I ran into any problems.

The next day and a half consisted of several meetings with the management team. I described the services we offered and pitched our proposal. The client agreed with most of my suggestions, and I felt we were building an excellent rapport. The next day we finished our meetings and business around noon.

The time had been well spent. I felt confident that we

would obtain the business. Things looked favorable. I now had three days before I had to be in Milwaukee. I grabbed a bite at a local diner and took the opportunity to scan the local paper. I always loved reading local news and getting history from different parts of the country, especially small towns.

Highway 52 took me north. It was still overcast, but having lived in the Midwest, the sixty degree temperature seemed very reasonable for this time of year. The drive was enjoyable and provided me with some valuable time to reflect on the events of the past month. I found myself praying that I would know what to say to help and comfort Carol, in her time of need.

It was not long before I began to notice billboards advertising the Field of Dreams. Although I had never been there, I couldn't help but weigh the significance of the name. In about six weeks my life had changed tremendously. A dream—this dream—had come to the forefront. I was now taking more chances and exploring avenues that a short time ago would have been off limits. I smiled. If this continues, I thought, I may try altering my salad dressing or even attempting to eat a burger without ketchup!

As I continued on the road , my thoughts once again turned to Carol. Had she been happy? Did she find fulfillment? Did things turn out as she had hoped for and anticipated? After all, it had been thirty-eight years.

Time changes so much. America? America was wholly different now. Eight more presidents had left their mark on the oval office. We were now in a deep recession. We had seen advancements in technology. Computers with the internet and cell phones brought the world into closer proximity. America had survived the terrorist attacks of 9/11, and was at war in Iraq and Afghanistan in an attempt to keep the world safe. Along the way babies were born and people died. We had seen several wars, a change of Popes, the bursting of a tech bubble. I found myself wondering whether Carol and I would be able to relate to each other. But, then again, hadn't her response demonstrated that she still remembered and had not forgotten our Romeo and Juliet?

Neither of us had attended class reunions. Why? Was it due to guilt? embarrassment? or an unconscious desire to leave the past untouched? Maybe it would be a car without tires, a bat without a ball, a Romeo without ... Yes, she had been my first love—my only love prior to Julie. It took me a long time to start dating again after my relationship ended with Carol. Then I met Julie. Even though I really thought she was a wonderful woman, it took me more than six months to get up the courage to ask her on a date. I wasn't looking for love, it found me.

I remembered an article I had previously read about 'first loves.' The author stated that many people try to forget their first love, because they fear future relationships may never live up to the excitement and passion of one's first romance. In essence, our first love can set us up for failure. The author went on to discuss that at some point after the honeymoon-period with our long-term spouse, many of us begin to wonder how life *might have been* with our first love.

We must remember that each relationship is unique, with its own set of circumstances.

I found myself reflecting on that article and have reached the conclusion that one's first relationship can set the tone for future relationships. People who had a nurturing first love experience seem to be more secure with their current partners. It makes sense. We learn from experience and try to duplicate the positive aspects as much as possible. Some people say that a first love may be a big key to the future, but it probably pales in comparison to a last, or lasting love. In reality, we prefer to recall positive experiences - good times, good friends, and that special feeling we felt in knowing that we were truly loved.

I soon approached a road sign - "Welcome to McCracken County." According to Carol, I should be arriving in McGregor in about ten minutes. I saw a turnoff for Pike's Peak State Park, just as she had described.

It was late afternoon and still overcast when I arrived in McGregor, and I was immediately enchanted with the quaint little town set right on the shores of the Mississippi River. McGregor had been established in 1837 and its population was approximately eight hundred residents. It was a nice vacation destination for fishermen and boaters. I learned the town was supported by commercial fishing, river boating, farming, grapes and even a casino. I quickly made my way up Main Street and found my accommodation, the Lamp Post Inn and Gallery. It was a charming Bed and Breakfast with a very cozy, homey appeal. I pulled in front and parked.

The owners, a pleasant retired couple, met me at the door. "You must be Jake. Come on in, and make yourself at home!" they stated. They warmly welcomed me and offered to take me on a tour of their beautiful home. The tour ended at my room, which would be my home for the next few days. After organizing my belongings, I laid for a moment on the bed. I said a short prayer, and thanked God for the opportunity that loomed ahead. I prayed for the strength to be supportive of Carol and asked the Lord to lead me down the right path. I prayed for the confidence to understand my role at this time, to be of service to Carol in her time of need.

After reflecting for almost an hour, I got up and decided to take a long walk. I took my time, enjoying a leisurely stroll. I must have walked at least a mile or more, witnessing the sights and sounds of Small Town America. I finally noticed a local establishment, Old Man River Restaurant and Brewery, and realized that I was very hungry. This would be a great place to have dinner.

The building had been built as an office around 1885 and was beautifully renovated. The manager, Andrew, a real history buff, struck up a conversation and was more than willing to share some of the town's prize stories with me. I was intrigued to find that the town's founder, Alexander McGregor had endured years of real estate litigation with his very own brother James. Appeals resulted and were heard at the Iowa supreme court. As a result, Alexander ended up being buried across the river in Prairie du Chien while James, his brother and worst enemy, was buried in McGregor. Even after their deaths the feud continued.

On a more pleasant note, I learned that the famous Ringling brothers had resided in McGregor. Four of brothers had been born here. As young men, they put on their own circus performances on a vacant lot beside their home. They later went on to purchase the Barnum & Bailey Circus in 1907, but ran the circuses separately until 1919.

Finally, Andrew told me about another McGregor resident, Andrew Clemens, famous for his sand art. As a young boy, Andrew Clemens lost his ability to speak and hear due to encephalitis. Never the less, with his own special tools he would pack sand tightly in various designs and paint scenes using multi-colored sands. One of his works was on display at the local library.

I appreciated Andrew's stories, but by the time my dinner arrived my attention and my mind were back on Carol and the task at hand. I had ordered the daily special, the roast beef dinner. It was tender and delicious, and true to small towns, very reasonably priced. With barely any room to spare, I still ordered a warm, thick slice of homemade cherry pie to end the enjoyable meal.

Back in my room, I called Julie and told her about my day. She told me that she was very tired from a very busy day at the hospital and intended to get to bed early.

"I love you, Jake. Good luck tomorrow," Julie said as she hung up the phone.

I then called Carol. She was pleased that I had made it safely. We agreed to meet at 9:00 a.m. at McGregor Coffee

Roasters, a coffee house a little closer to her side of town.

After hanging up the phone, I lay there quietly. Tomorrow would be a very interesting day. Thirty-eight years? Would she even recognize me? The very thought of seeing her made me nervous. As I began to fall asleep, I could hear the distant whistle of a train as it made its way through town. It was a sound that I had not heard for many, many years. I remember thinking, Carol too must be hearing this same sound being only a short distance up the road as she lay in her slumber. I began to wonder. Would I meet Carol in the park again tonight in my dreams?

I certainly did.

Chapter Eight

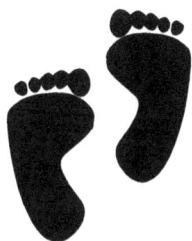

Birk

I woke to a peaceful scenario—brilliant sunlight and birds chirping outside my window. At the same time, I immediately felt queasy and apprehensive. What would be Carol's first response? Should I shake her hand? give her a hug? a kiss? I had the guts to call her to begin with, so I could certainly handle this, right? A kiss would be the respectful thing to do.

I showered and got ready. The proprietors greeted me and offered breakfast, but I declined. Our nine o'clock meeting was less than an hour away. McGregor's Coffee Roasters was just minutes up the road. I had known that I would not be able to eat anything before, and had purposely left myself little time. I decided to make a brief stop at St Paul's Lutheran Church. I prayed for Carol and that I would be able to help her in her grief. I lit a candle for her. As I was leaving I ran directly into the church minister. Reverend Bill smiled and introduced himself to me. I asked him if he had a few moments for me. I explained that I was here from out of state to aid a friend. I asked him if he would mind saying a short prayer for my intentions so that I could assist her to the best of my ability. Reverend Bill put his hand on my shoulder and prayed for me. He prayed that I could be an instrument of God and that I would find the strength and courage to persevere in my attempt to assist Carol. It was a very touching and moving prayer which left me filled with confidence and a strong sense of duty.

I thanked Reverend Bill for his blessing.

"The Lord be with you, my son." he replied.

Despite my stop at church, I arrived a good twenty-five minutes early. The hostess seated me in the corner booth I requested. I told her that in about a half an hour a woman would join me.

She laughed. "Aren't you lucky!" she said.

I scanned the menu, and decided on a cup of coffee. The smell of fresh brewed coffee permeated the air. The anticipation was overwhelming. I shut my eyes, uttered another short prayer. My stop at church had given me a boost of confidence. However, for a moment I briefly thought back to the time in the park thirty-eight years earlier when Carol never came.

About nine on the dot, I looked out the window and saw a woman get out of a car. She had shoulder length light blonde hair and was wearing a yellow sweater. She approached the front door, and soon stood before the hostess station. At once, she glanced over in my direction, and spotted me. She smiled, and made her way over.

I got up, gave her a hug, and then delivered a kiss on her cheek.

"Carol—it is so great to see you again!"

"Jake, you look—great!"

She slipped into her side of the booth, and I into mine. For a moment we simply looked at each other.

"And thank you so much for that sympathy card you sent. I really do appreciate it."

"You're certainly welcome."

Suddenly I was at a loss for words. It was just like the

first day I had met her in the hall at school and had decided on a quick exit. I hoped that she could make me feel at ease as she had always done in the past.

"You know, Jake, life is fickle. Life is full of twists and turns. I'm beginning to realize that, and for the first time I'm trying to make decisions just for my—"

"Sir, would you like a refill?" interrupted the waitress, "and what would your wife like to drink?"

Carol gave her a double take, but said nothing. Then, "I'll ... have some raspberry tea, please," she said.

The waitress nodded, then departed. Carol peered up again. "So how do you like our little town? I'll bet it's a little more rural then you are used to."

"Honestly, it reminds me of where we grew up in Wisconsin."

"Yes, I know, that's ... why I love it so much." She was silent for a moment, then said, "Jake, I really want to thank you for coming. I was so depressed, in such bad shape. You really gave me a spark."

She looked at me, shrugged oddly, then asked about my family. For the next fifteen minutes I expounded about Julie and our children. I gave her a play-by-play—everything since leaving college. As my story unfolded, I took her in. Her smile was radiant. It hadn't changed in all these years. Again she was making me feel secure, giving me a shot of timely confidence. This prompted me to keep talking. Before long, I found myself sharing some of the truly funny and wacky things that had occurred in the past years as well. Amid these stories she laughed, and shook her head. Her once-familiar gestures became recognizable all over again.

It was then her turn. She ran with the ball, telling some truly funny stories and outdoing me by adding funny voices and crazy gestures as only she could do. I couldn't help but laugh and at the same time think back to those amazing times from high school. It was amazing how alike our families were. We both had sent our kids to parochial grade schools, then to public high schools. Her kids, too, were very athletic and participated on many sports teams. Her daughter Susan played the clarinet just like my Lucy. Her kids and ours had gone to college. Her oldest had a master's degree. Their family even belonged to the local Lutheran church with the same name as ours. How ironic it was the same church I had stumbled upon this morning. Everyone in her family was relatively successful, stable, and happy. Our lives had virtually mirrored each other.

I told her she must have been a great mom, and she replied, "Thanks Jake. And I know you were a terrific dad."

For a moment a silence hung. Then she sighed audibly, and began.

"Jake, I want to tell you what happened. About a year ago Jim's business started to go downhill. It was right after he had taken a large loan to purchase some machinery. Well, orders started falling off and sales started to drop significantly. Within six months we had to lay off twelve people—relatives and life-long friends. It was horrible. Jim felt so bad about it, and we took a home-equity loan to bolster the business.

We never should have. Soon our home value dropped and we found ourselves teetering on collapse. It all ... just got the best of him. On February 25—right at work—he had a massive coronary. They rushed him to the hospital. His brother called me. I hurried over. I was too late. By twenty minutes. We ... never got a chance to say goodbye."

She sat silently for a moment. I caught a slight tear in her eye. I couldn't help but think that Jim had died the same day as my first dream.

"Carol, I am so very, very sorry. Jim sounds like a great guy. I mean—he had to be to marry you. We know that he is now with God. We just need to put our faith in the Lord more than ever. He is walking by you, and with you. It is going to be okay. I promise."

She managed a smile, gently patted my hand. "Jake, can you follow me? I want to show you our home."

"Absolutely. I'd love to see it."

The next thing I knew I was following her through town. I could see she still had a lead foot. We came to a particularly attractive, very wooded part of town. She turned into the driveway of a rustic, two-story home. I couldn't believe my eyes. Just as when I had first known her, again she lived in the woods. It was as if she had transformed her previous lot back in Wisconsin to Iowa. I guess she never lost her love of nature. Before I could comment, I noticed a 'For Sale' sign advertising on the lawn. I knew right then it would be very difficult for her to give up such a significant part of her existence. Losing Jim and then suffering the loss of her home would be devastating. I felt a slight tug in my stomach.

We walked to the front door. Several empty flowerpots and two rocking chairs sat on the front porch. Inside, to the left was her dining room, to the right her sunken living room. We stepped into the dining room and there on the wall hung a picture of her parents.

"You remember Mom and Dad? They passed, years ago. I really miss both of them."

I remembered the two wonderful people. They had always treated me kindly. I had always felt they would make terrific in-laws. I knew they were with God now and hopefully her dad was catching some big fish in heaven, even as we spoke. At once, I felt sad, because we had enjoyed a wonderful relationship years ago. With the way our lives and relationships had re-structured and played out, I had never known of their passing.

We moved into the kitchen. I could see that she was a very neat and tidy homemaker. In high school, I remembered Carol telling me that she intended to have a very orderly kitchen. She had predicted well. We moved into the family room. In the corner of the room was an old pair of men's sneakers. "I guess I … need to be getting rid of these sometime soon," she said.

Her backyard showed through the family-room patio doors. The grass outside was very matted and wet, since the snow had only recently melted. In one corner of the lot was a dilapidated tree house that had enjoyed better times.

The family room was filled with photos. The kids'

resemblance to her was amazing. I could see they loved baseball and basketball and that one of the boys had caught a very large fish.

We made our way back to the living room and its exquisite fireplace. She looked at me kind of oddly, and said, "Here— is our wedding picture."

I stared at the picture. My breath grew short. My heart raced. I felt my jaw drop and tried to catch my breath. There was Carol in her wedding gown, standing—beside the man at the picnic table, the *man* in my dreams!

I stood by, numbed. At once a tangible cool chill ran down my spine. All thoughts of me, a shadow personality, and growth seemed out the window. This totally unexpected occurrence had not only knocked me for a loop, but had served to scare the heck out of me.

It was definitely a new ball game. I now faced a new and unfamiliar realm—one which was truly out of my comfort zone. Was this the new age of psychic phenomena? I did not know how to react.

"Are you—all right, Jake?"

She was eyeing me with genuine concern.

"Uh, fine. Fine," with a slight rasp in my voice.

The numbness ebbed; sensation once again returned to my body.

"Fine," I said again. "I ... I'm so sorry, Carol."

"Thank you for coming to my home, Jake."

The room at once grew oppressive. Again my breath came in starts. I asked Carol if she would like to go to lunch.

"Great," she answered. I then suggested we take one car. "Thank you, Jake, that way we can continue to visit." she added.

Outside I asked, "So you are going to sell?"

"Yes. Jim's insurance wasn't quite enough. I'm going to be downsizing a little. It's okay, though. I'm an empty nester now anyway."

The restaurant she suggested was at the Marina, right on the Mississippi. She told me that Jim really loved this place. The view was spectacular. We had talked incessantly, like old friends. Indeed, we were. Toward the meal's end she said, "Jake, I really appreciate what you said—I mean, that everything is going to be okay. It made me feel better. You … always had a way of making me feel better."

"I hoped it would," I said.

After lunch, Carol said, "I want to show you a special spot on this very special day. It is one in a million."

"I'm game. Let's go."

We drove back through town and arrived at Pikes Peak State Park.

"Okay, please turn in here. Then make your first left."

We drove down an old winding dirt road for about a quarter of a mile. We came to a parking area, and stopped. How weird, I thought. After all these years, here we were in a park together! We got out, walked through a wooded area for a few minutes, and reached a clearing.

"Let's sit here."

We sat down beside each other at a picnic table, viewing

nature's beauty all around.

After a few minutes of silence Carol walked me over to a spot that had a gorgeous view of the Mississippi. "This was Jim's and my most favorite spot," she said after a time. "In fact this overlook, it's ... where he proposed to me. I just wanted you to see it."

"It's very beautiful. Almost as if we are close to God," I replied.

"That's just what he would say. You are really a wonderful person, Jake. You have lifted my spirits. Thank you for coming here with me today—thank you."

We both walked back to the picnic table and sat silently for a few moments, taking in the view and feeling the energy that only nature can provide. It started to drizzle ever so slightly and the clouds looked ominous. At once Carol stood and smiled.

"Jake—how would you like to go to a church retreat with me? It's tomorrow. Could you join me?"

I nodded.

With that, she started walking down a path towards the woods. All at once I began to cry uncontrollably. My dream; I was reliving it. First, her husband? And now her request?

Carol called to me. "Jake—are you ... Uh, follow me. I know a shortcut back to the car. We can stay dry."

I hastened to catch up and to avoid the rain which was now starting to come down much heavier. As I glanced down at the dirt path I could see her footprints on the moist soil. Beside her prints were other larger ones. For every print she left, there seemed another larger one—every step of the way.

At her house I simply dropped her off. We agreed that I would pick her up at 9:30 in the morning. Together we would attend the retreat in nearby Strawberry Point. The town was about an hour away. It would be a beautiful drive.

She told me to dress warmly, since many of the activities were scheduled to be held outdoors.

Chapter Nine

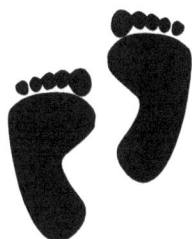

I was exhausted. It had been an emotional day for both of us and I was feeling its effects. I sat propped on the edge of the bed, head in hands, mystified. I simply could not explain. The resemblance of the man in my dream to Carol's husband? The picnic table and the church retreat? Further confirmations? The only thing left was the message I hoped to find. Ms. Tarver had sure been accurate when she advised us not to worry if we don't fully understand our dreams, that somehow God would take care of the rest. Was it God who was holding my hand, clearing this path for me? Each step of the way, it seems that I have been led by the Lord's hand. From the dream itself... to the dream class at school... the dream analyst... the call to Carol... Ben's sudden jury duty and the need for me to replace him... seeing Carol again... viewing her wedding picture and finally... Carol asking me to attend the retreat. Was this a pre-conceived path? What lay in store for me tomorrow?

After about an hour of wearied thinking, I checked my watch. Julie would be home now. I gave her a call, and told her everything. She was flabbergasted, and could not believe what had transpired.

"Honey, this whole thing is just too *strange*," she said. "Please be *careful*. You're right. This whole thing *does* seem to be unraveling like some bizarre book. Let's pray it has a happy ending. Again, Darling, Please be *careful*. Know that I love you dearly!"

After a few minutes I headed out for supper. This time I took the car. I decided to go back to Old Man River. The folks remembered me from the previous night and Andrew greeted me with a smile. I told them the food and hospitality had been so good that I had no choice but to come back again.

Once again, Andrew felt a need to relate another story. He told me an elaborate story about a woman from McGregor, Emma Eastman, who was married at least nine times. He said the town folks referred to her as the 'Virgin Em'. Some claim the number of her husbands was actually ten. Rumor had it Em would boast to neighbors that she hoped to make it a dozen. There are tales that if she was angry with a husband, she would send him to the cemetery to whitewash the headstones of her former spouses, perhaps to give them a preview of 'what was to come'? Even when she was up in age she continued to remarry. Andrew said that even though there were some doubters, rumor had it she was only married to one person at a time. This he related with slight chuckle in his voice. It was a one-of-its-kind story that left me laughing as well.

I enjoyed a delicious dinner of fish and chips. On my way out the door, Andrew made one last remark with his eyebrows raised, "By the way Jake, I once heard there was a sign in our city hall that stated 'McGregor, built on a bluff and run the same way!'" Andrew smiled and we both laughed. I drove back slowly and went right to bed.

Again I dreamed. This time it became crystal clear that I *was* in Pike's Peak State Park with Carol. Again she smiled at me. Again she asked me to attend the retreat. Then swiftly I found myself whisked away to a drive-in movie when we were seventeen, *Gone With the Wind*. I remember that we were both so bored—such a long movie. However, we did make the best of it. For several weeks after, whenever she would pose a question, I would respond with, "Frankly, Carol, my dear, *I don't give a damn!*"

Even before the wake-up call, the birds were at it again, chirping vigorously, as if signaling me to get up and get ready. It was another beautiful morning, with brilliant sunshine filtering through the sheer window treatments. I showered, got dressed, and headed to the dining area for a cup of coffee and to read the local paper.

About 9:15 I drove to Carol's. As I pulled in, I noticed another, smaller car in the driveway. I rang the doorbell. A young blonde girl opened the door.

"Hello, I'm Susan, Carol's daughter. You must be Jake? I've heard so much about you. I remember seeing you in Mom's high-school yearbook. You guys went to prom and homecoming together. Please come in."

"A pleasure to meet you, Susan."

She smiled. "I'll see what's keeping Mom."

I couldn't believe it. Susan looked so much like a youthful Carol—very beautiful and with the same engaging smile. It was like I had stepped back in time to 1970.

In the living room all alone, I walked over to take a better look at Carol's wedding picture, almost hoping that the male figure had changed overnight, or that maybe I had imagined the whole thing. No such luck. The same figure stared back at me!

I could hear them coming down the stairs. Carol appeared, rushed over and greeted me with a surprising kiss on the cheek. With Susan there, I felt a little embarrassed.

Carol looked wonderful. I could tell she had taken ample time to get ready.

"Jake, I've got to show you this cardinal that has been in our back yard for the last few weeks. He's *beautiful*."

As we stepped into the family room and neared the patio doors, she noticed the sneakers again. This time they appeared to be caked with fresh mud.

"Funny. I don't remember them being so dirty yesterday. But, Jake—look."

Yes, the cardinal was beautiful. I told her it was a sign of good fortune to come. She smiled and announced that we had to get going if we were to make it to Strawberry on time.

As we left, Susan remarked, "You guys have a great time. And Jake—her curfew is eleven p.m. sharp!"

"Yes, ma'am," I smiled.

It was already about 65 degrees. The sun was shining brilliantly. The drive was enticing, with trees just starting to bud. This part of Iowa was extremely picturesque, especially in the spring. The drive brought back memories of our time as teenagers in Wisconsin. Today Carol seemed happier, which made me feel better.

We didn't talk much, but that was fine. I know she was contemplating, among other things, the retreat. She glanced to me several times, each time with a smile. The silence held.

Finally, I could take it no more.

"I know what you're thinking."

She looked to me oddly. "What?"

"You're thinking about the time at prom, when we got stuck in the mud at Ann's house."

Her frown turned quickly into laughter.

"I *still* can't believe what Dan said."

I grinned. "If we get stuck today, don't worry Carol, I am equipped with Triple A and a cell phone," I emphasized, and she laughed even more.

She then told me about Reverend Dave, whom she had known for more than thirty years, whom I would meet today. "Originally, he was our pastor at our church in McGregor," she explained. "Reverend Dave is like a brother to me. He is such a kind soul. I just love him. Even when he was a child he wanted to become a minister. He just had that calling."

Our trip took us southwest towards Strawberry Point.

I said to Carol, "I have to say Carol, Strawberry Point sounds like a city that is right up your alley."

Carol laughed and proceeded to tell me that the city is the home of the world's largest strawberry. "We will see it as we drive through town. Each summer there is a strawberry festival and the strawberries are not only abundant but huge. Each year our whole family made the trip and picked enough to last for the summer and into the fall. You know how much I like my strawberries and raspberries!" she added.

Sure enough, as I made my way through town, the giant strawberry appeared. Carol and I both smiled. With moderate traffic and Carol's perfect directions, it took just over an hour. The retreat was actually at a summer camp just outside of town. There was a small church on the grounds. We parked the car and as we registered, she started to pay. But I insisted.

She then introduced me to Reverend Dave, who gave her a big hug. He turned to me. "You must be the fellow who has come all the way from Arizona?"

"That would be me."

He smiled, shook my hand, and welcomed me. "I'm so glad that you will be joining us today." he added.

I was getting very positive vibes. I couldn't put my finger on it, but I suspected that this place was significant and that this experience might reveal the missing answers.

With the attendees gathered, we began singing "Amazing Grace." At the song's conclusion, Reverend Dave stepped up into the pulpit and began to speak. He was not only a minister but a certified grief counselor. As he spoke, his staff handed out literature.

The Reverend thanked everyone for taking the time to come today to this special day of reflection. He reminded us that with God in our lives, everything is possible. "Brothers and sisters–let's unite in love," he suggested, and emphasized the special purpose of this retreat—to helping those grieving the end of relationships. He went on to say that people come here for diverse reasons—recent deaths, divorces, and just to commemorate those who have passed but are still deeply embedded in our hearts. "We welcome all of you with open arms. We accept you unconditionally," he said.

He provided us with the day's agenda. The retreat would begin with an opening prayer service and lecture by Pastor Nelson. Afterwards, we would break into groups of four or five to discuss our own unique situation, if we so chose. The men would go to the recreation center and the women would remain in the church. We were encouraged to share as we felt the need, and to the extent that we were able. The group meeting was expected to last for one hour. Everyone would have the opportunity to tell their stories. Afterwards, we would re-convene as a group.

Once the entire group was back together, Pastor Nelson would ask for volunteers to share not only what each had learned from the others, but to identify the action steps that had helped them better cope with their loss.

Afterwards, we would then break for lunch and fellowship for about an hour. Following lunch, we would be asked to choose a partner for a fifteen minute one on one discussion. We were encouraged to choose someone we felt we could bond with. In this exercise, we would be asked to identify and share with our chosen partner the one thing that still bothers us and hurts us deep inside, something hard for us to accept. The partner's role is to offer suggestions and assistance. After this short, but important segment, we would conclude the day with a prayer service in the chapel.

To begin, we recited the Lord's Prayer. As we did so, we all held hands, even across the pews and aisles. Carol took my hand, held it firmly. Her touch felt warm. Her skin was soft, just as I had remembered. As we ended, she gave my hand a slight squeeze, and smiled. I returned the smile.

After another hymn, "Let There Be Peace on Earth," and a reading, Pastor Nelson took the podium. He was a very tall man with long hair and a full beard, resembling my impression of a Jesus look-alike. He was scheduled to speak for about a half an hour on the topic "Grief and our path to healing." The Pastor was known to be a dynamic speaker. He began by saying, "I would like to thank you all for coming today. Simply by virtue of you being here today, you are taking steps towards your emotional wellness. I applaud you."

Pastor Nelson then explained that grief is actually a very complex process. In fact, grief manifests in seven different stages. He further described the seven stages. The first stage is disbelief. This can be associated with a numbness we feel just after hearing dreadful news. The next stage is denial. In this stage, we do not want to believe or cannot accept what has happened. We feel that it just can't be real. The third stage is negotiation. Here we have thoughts of trying to make a deal with God or even destiny in an attempt to buy more time with the loved one. This stage is then followed by guilt, where we wish we could have done more for the departed but no longer have the opportunity. This leads to the anger stage. Here a person may start to think in selfish terms such as—how could the deceased have left us all alone? To be abandoned like this just isn't fair! This easily breeds the depression stage. Depression is a normal reaction to losing a loved one, can lead to a number of issues and is the most critical stage. Finally, there is acceptance. Here we finally feel some resolution to the death and attempt to go on with our lives.

I wondered where Carol's mind was in the scheme of all this. Would this information better equip me to help her? Pastor Nelson emphasized that people don't go through these stages in any particular order. They can be in and out of stages in short periods of time. Often stress prompts those left behind to adopt certain aspects of the deceased person's illness. They may have a tendency to withdraw. Crying is normal and can be positive as we learn to deal with our new circumstance. It can be a good thing to look back on such fond memories—photos, trips, family times, special gifts that identify the deceased. If we can't eat, sleep, or even concentrate, we should see a physician or therapist. We all need to know that grief has a beginning and an end. Time does heal. Most importantly, no two people are alike. Everyone will go through the stages of grief in their own unique way.

"Remember to do special things for yourself," he advised. "Go to a ball game. Get a massage. Get out of the house. Be sure to eat properly. Surround yourselves with friends and loved ones. Those here today in support of someone grieving, we thank you for your love and support."

At this, Carol once again squeezed my hand and smiled.

"Your caring is an integral part of the healing process. Simply being with that person is a sign of your support and caring. The faster a person can surround himself with loving friends, the faster he can accelerate the healing process. Don't be afraid to talk about the deceased. It can be very beneficial to share loving, happy memories."

In closing, the Pastor said, "Love is like a great tsunami, an overpowering force of nature. We love very deep. It is the depth of our love that makes the grieving process even more difficult to go through. Remember my dear people, there is an end to this grieving process. Consider this: It is better to have loved and lost than never to have loved at all."

The Pastor half-bowed, to a round of applause. It was apparent that we had enjoyed his lecture and had concentrated on his every word.

We commenced to break into our groups. "I'll see you a little later," I called. "I'll be here waiting for you," Carol replied.

The gathering had over two hundred people, almost evenly divided between men and women. There were about twenty groups at each location. My group consisted of five— three older men, one younger man who had recently lost his wife to cancer, and me. The others were very forthcoming, all willing to share their stories.

The three elders spoke first. Adam had been married to Ellen for more than forty years. She had died six months earlier. He missed her dearly. He thought about her each day. Each week he would visit her grave and talk to her. Having such a relationship with her now was his way to cope.

John had been married for fifteen years, his second

marriage. He had been divorced for many years before finding and marrying Ann, who had died recently. He missed Ann a great deal, but he felt that his experience with his first wife had provided him with a built-in mechanism to cope with losing a spouse. He was very lonely, he confessed. He said he would never marry again.

It was then Frank's turn. He was forthright and admitted that his wife had found another man to love. Unbeknown to him, she had been seeing this other man for a long time. Finally one day, she asked for a divorce. Frank was devastated. He lost his faith in the Lord, lost his way. It was going on eight weeks and he knew that he needed to address the problem. We all felt very bad for him. He had no control of the situation, and it was causing him great anxiety. He went on. Immediately he had felt betrayal, anger, shock, hopelessness. As he spoke, I could envision what he had gone through. It was what I had felt years ago, when Carol told me she didn't want to see me any longer. Frank told the group he did not feel that the other significant people in his life understood the depths of his grief. Initially, he didn't want to go on anymore. Through many sleepless nights he wondered what he could have done better. But now he realized the time had come to realize that the relationship with his wife was, in fact, over. He had to move forward. As he spoke, I realized that I began to cry. He continued. He identified that attending this retreat was a very big first step on his healing journey. He decided to join a support group and return to church soon. He intended to read self-help books. And Reverend Dave?

The Reverend had been a godsend. "Reverend Dave told me the importance of reaching out. Consequently, you will find strength, joy, healing, and love in the midst of all the chaos in your life. I just need to walk with the Lord."

Next was William, a very young twenty-eight year old, whose wife of the same age had succumbed quickly to breast cancer and left him to care for their two-year-old. He missed her so much. It had been eight months, and this was the first time he had been anywhere by himself. His mom was watching his son Phillip. He thanked everyone for listening.

When my turn came, I didn't feel my dream was worth mentioning, so I said that I was here just to help an old friend whose spouse had passed away. The group however, was very interested in my story. What brought me here today? Adam on my right asked me if I had ever lost a partner in my lifetime? I told him, yes, I had—about thirty-eight years ago, someone I had loved very much.

"Did she die?" he asked.

"You could say so."

"Well you certainly must know how to cope since you have made it this long."

I thought for a moment. "Yes, I guess I must," I agreed.

We all hit it off. By the end of our session we had become close teammates in our fight against grieving. Our group was cohesive and dynamic, and I felt I had gained some valuable wisdom I could use to help Carol. I also seemed to have gained some insight into my own issues. As we concluded our time together we gave each other hugs as a sign of unity.

I felt like I was a part of team of some sort. God's team?

When our time was over, we all gathered as a group back at the chapel. I found Carol and we again sat together. Several folks stood up and offered their own personal stories and what they were doing each day to survive their ordeals.

Virtually all who spoke admitted that they had helpless feelings at the deaths of their spouses. The biggest issue seemed to be lack of control of their destiny. The divorced felt that they had some control in the situation, some choice in the matter. But the loss of a spouse prompted great disappointment, sorrow, even regret. Many times the role of the partners was an issue in itself. If the spouse was the breadwinner or the one making the majority of the decisions, it could cause great anxiety. On the other hand, if the spouse was the one who took care of the home, it presented a whole new set of issues. Simply, these people had formed bonds long ago which now, for purposes of their earthly lives, were over.

Several suggested that we be sure to see a doctor and have a mental check-up regularly. Many felt a bond with our group, now that they realized that they were not the only ones with a grief issue.

The session was dynamic, productive, and left everyone still talking as we broke for lunch. Lunches in hand, Carol and I found a picnic table several trees beyond the farthest group.

"Jake, I think I'd just rather sit by ourselves for a few minutes—if you don't mind."

"That's fine, no problem at all."

As we ate, she seemed nervous and distraught. Had the session been too much for her? Or maybe just a little too early?

"Carol, did you ever write that book that you wanted to write?" I asked.

She gave me a curious look.

"You know—the one about the uniqueness of family and the eternal promise of hope? You always told me that you felt the most important thing in life was family. You also said that no matter what circumstances present themselves, we must treat each day as a new day and therefore we must always possess the 'promise of hope'."

Rather startled, she looked at me. "I … did say that to you in our driveway one night. After we lost to that team from Milwaukee in basketball!"

"Exactly. But then, after a while you brought it down to my level. You referred to our team at school as 'the family' and our next opportunity or 'promise of hope'–Tuesday against Brookfield East High!"

She laughed. "I'm *going* to write that book, Jake. I am. Thanks for the reminder."

Reverend Dave then announced that it was time to find partners for the fifteen-minute sessions. Carol looked to me. "Can I please be your partner, Jake?" she said.

I nodded, and gathered our lunch trash and disposed of it in a trash can. I sat back down, and decided to take the lead.

"Carol, where two or more are gathered in His name,

God will be there too. Let's say the Lord's prayer. To start off."

We held hands, we recited the prayer.

"Okay, Carol, please tell me the thing that you cannot accept about your situation. The one thing that hurts you the most."

Her smile disappeared. She just looked at me with a look of desperation.

"Jake, I told you yesterday. My biggest issue is that Jim and I never got a chance to say goodbye."

At once she started to cry, uncontrollably. She sniffled, and continued.

"Jake, I feel *such* a pain in my heart. Right now."

I felt so sad for her. I rose, walked awkwardly across to her side of the table, bent, and draped my arms around her. I told her that she was loved. *Very* loved. I held her tight.

"Carol, it's okay. Don't be afraid to cry. You couldn't get there in time. You tried. Jim knows it wasn't your fault. He loves you and very well might have wanted to spare you all that added grief. Sometimes events occur that we have no control over. God works in mysterious ways. Our ways are not His ways. We need to trust in Him. Remember the story of The Footprints in the Sand? Often when we are at our lowest and feel we are walking all alone—the most difficult times—we see only one set of footprints. We assume that they are our own. In reality they are Jesus', who is carrying us. Carol, trust in the Lord. He'll help you find your way. He loves you. I love you. Your family loves you. You are strong and wonderful and dynamic and have much left to accomplish on this earth. Carol, if someone leaves you— don't lose faith!"

Brushing away the tears, she looked up. There was a noticeable quiver in her voice. "Thanks Jake," she said. "Just how did you get so good at this?"

"Oh, I guess I've had a little practice along the way."

We sat silent for several minutes. At once came the announcement—"Two minutes."

She held me tightly, as if she did not want to let go. She was literally shaking. All of a sudden she stared up. "So what is the one thing that you cannot accept in life? What hurts *you* the most?"

I looked at her for about five seconds and finally said, "Carol, I could never accept that you would ever be in pain."

With this, I began to sob myself. For a moment I wanted to tell her that we really shared the same issue. My not being able to say goodbye to her years ago had devastated me. But no, I couldn't tell her. This was her time. This was not about me. She had just lost the love of her life.

She began to cry again. I held her. People were filing by, looking.

"We've need to get to the service," I lamented.

We stood up and slowly walked together, and sat down in the back of the church. The service included several songs including one of my favorites, "Here I Am, Lord."

Reverend Dave took the pulpit for his closing remarks.

He left us with the following insight. "Remember, as you make your way forth, you are walking hand and hand with the Lord. You need to adopt Jesus as your life partner. He will always be there for you with His *unconditional* love."

The service concluded with a music-accompanied meditation, with the lights turned down. The last hymn, "We Are Called," was very emotionally soothing, allowing us some time to reflect on the day's events. Carol held my arm the whole while, even as we said our final goodbyes to everyone. Reverend Dave thanked me for coming and told me to have a safe trip back. "Don't hesitate to come back," he said. "We have many repeaters."

I shook his hand warmly, firmly, and said goodbye. He was a rare, incredible person. For some reason I felt that I had known him all my life.

It was only when we reached the car that Carol released my arm. I could tell that she was very upset and sad. As soon as we got in she reached over, again took my arm, held it tight, and fell fast asleep.

The lights of the house were dark. I didn't wake her until we got well into the driveway. She needed all the rest she could muster, after all she had gone through today.

When she woke she seemed happier.

"Jake, don't go. Please come in for a little while."

Inside, we walked back into the kitchen.

"Let's have some tea."

She moved into the family-room area to light a fire, but didn't have much success.

"Jake—can you help me please?"

"Certainly."

I prepared the fire as she fetched the tea.

We both sat and enjoyed our tea, of course—raspberry, her favorite. We sat and talked, and she laid her head on my shoulder. Just like years ago, at the end of her driveway. We relived some wonderful times. How easy and carefree times seemed back then! We talked about *Wait Until Dark* and coming home to a house without lights and calling the police. We talked about how she should have opted for the raspberry shake and forgotten about the legendary Black Cow. I told her that I wished that she could have played high-school basketball, especially with her unbelievable shot. She laughed. She got more than enough enjoyment watching and cheering for me, she said.

"O.K. Carol," I said, "What do you guess is my all-time favorite movie?"

She chuckled and replied, "That's pretty easy Jake, it's got to be *Hoosiers*."

"Amazing," I said, "simply amazing!"

"And what is mine Jake? she said with a curious look.

I took a second and then raised my eyebrows. "You have the same favorite as you always did. It is still *The Wizard of Oz*." With that said we both smiled and seemed to be gauging the other's reaction.

I then asked her to tell me more about Jim, if she wanted. Once she started in about Jim and the family, she sparked up. Carol told me about how religious he was. "Jim was like

a saint in his thoughts and actions. We went to church every
week. He was an usher and a the leader of the choir. In the
summer he played on the church softball team and he was in
charge of our July church festival for the last five years."

Carol told me that each summer, more than a few times,
several families from their church would rent boats and
venture to a part of the Mississippi River that had a very
large sand bar. Here they would all stay for hours basking
in the cool waters and enjoying each other's company. They
all referred to this excursion as "Gilligan's Island." She then
told me about their trip to Florida the family took when the
kids were quite young and about each child's birth and how
she had been rushed to the hospital for her youngest, Susan.

Two years ago, she and Jim finally got to go on the cruise
in the Bahamas they had dreamed of for years. Carol told me
that every year on their anniversary they visited the overlook
at Pike's Peak Park where he had proposed. She then told
me that yesterday, when we had been in the park, had been
their anniversary. She told me several more stories about Jim
and what a wonderful man he was. The necklace she was
wearing? Jim had given it to her on her fifty-fifth birthday, a
few years ago. She would never take it off, she said.

We talked about what the future might hold. We talked of
better tomorrows, that we both must live our lives for today.

Suddenly her eyes rounded. "Jake—are you hungry?
I'm going to make you what you will probably consider 'the
world's greatest hamburger.'"

While she was in the kitchen, I threw another large log

on the fire. It didn't take long before we enjoyed a wonderful dinner.

"I bet you would like catsup with that—right?"

"Actually," I said, "I think I'm going to try it plain this evening. I am going to live on the wild side."

I had remembered correctly. The burgers were fantastic. They were the world's greatest.

We finished and cleaned up. Again we sat down comfortably. Again she laid her head on my shoulder and held my hand. We continued to talk about the little things in life that meant so much to each of us. After all these years we had not lost our ability to talk. I had thought it could never be the same. I guess you never know what tomorrow will bring.

We must have sat there for hours. It reminded me of high school and my favorite times with her. What a fitting time for our last night together! As the hour grew late, our conversations trailed off. I knew very well that she would have a tough road ahead. Already she had told me of the pain she felt when she was at home herself for the first time two weeks ago after Jim's death. The pain of realizing— finally—that now you are by yourself, that your loved one would never be returning. I felt deeply for her.

Then suddenly, as if someone had flicked the driveway lights on and off, I knew it was time. "Carol, I … really need to go," I said.

We stood. Her eyes, I noticed, were as red and welling as were mine. We edged to the door. There I turned and gave her a long kiss, a big hug.

"Jake, thank you for all you have done for me. I'll never forget it. I love you so very much." She hesitated for a second, then said, "Jake—I just can't say goodbye to you."

With tears in my eyes, I said, "I understand that it's difficult, but always know that I love you very much." I wiped a tear. "And make sure you work on that book. Definitely a best-seller!"

She smiled. I took a final deep breath and kissed her one last time on the cheek.

"Let's make it easy for each other." I looked deep into her eyes for a moment, my arms on her shoulders. "Wherefore art thou, Carol?" I said.

She managed another smile amid her tears. "Wherefore art thou, Jake."

I turned, slipped out, closed the door behind me. I knew the odds. I would most probably never see her again. But this time I had the opportunity—my chance to tell her just how much I loved her, my chance to finally say goodbye.

Chapter Ten

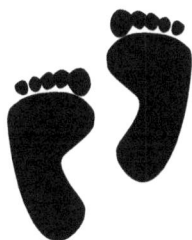

Back at the motel I called Julie and told her about the day. She could tell I was exhausted, that the ordeal had been emotional. She advised me to go right to bed. I did. This time I dreamed of Carol, but only briefly. Just as I had with Ms. Tarver, I only remembered the colors of blue and yellow and a sense of peace, love, joy, and happiness.

I awoke early, grabbed a quick bite to eat. With my morning coffee sitting in the holder next to me, I settled in for the long drive to Milwaukee. I started out heading north, to catch the bridge over the Mississippi into Wisconsin. I hadn't been back to Wisconsin in years. As it was right on the way, I drove past Carol's house one last time, just as the sun was starting to peek out. The house was dark. There was no movement. I pulled over and stopped. For a moment I just sat and thanked the Lord for my time here.

Once again I couldn't help but consider the placement of Carol's home—directly in the woods. Ever since I had known Carol she had lived in this setting, a location of mystery, a kind of hiding place. It seemed to me that there must be some aspect of her personality or even mine that I had overlooked or hadn't come to grips with. Maybe there had been unresolved feelings. However, I sure felt I now owned an unshakable faith in the Divine and felt totally at peace. Maybe I could finally see the forest for the trees.

A difficult task lie ahead for Carol. She would live life with a different vision, like a baby starting to take her first steps, with the very real possibility of falling. If she did fall,

I prayed it would be right into Jesus' arms. Again I said a prayer for Carol's intentions, as always. I prayed that in time she would soon enjoy life and better tomorrows, that soon she would be dancing with Jesus. I then drove away.

The sun was coming up hugely as I made my way onto the bridge. I couldn't help but think of the symbolism here. Rivers have carried people's dreams since the beginning of time. Rivers represent the eternal change in our lives. This mighty river does, in fact, emulate the way I have tried to live my life—with strength, power, courage, conviction. A bridge is a transition and signifies that I had not only the strength to complete this journey, but the boldness to move forward in my life. Somehow I had been given the opportunity to go back in time to help with a friend's healing, and to be healed myself. Now, after thirty-eight years, my journey was coming to an end.

As I reached the other side of the bridge, I was now in Prairie du Chien, Wisconsin. I turned and glanced back towards Iowa. It was then I realized that Carol had chosen her path and crossed her bridge over her river thirty-eight years before. It just happened to be in the *opposite* direction. And me? In a matter of some seven weeks life had turned me upside down and changed me significantly. I had gone from a skeptic to one of mild curiosity, to one owning a sure conviction concerning the power of dreams. I seemed to have grown spiritually, and felt great peace in my heart. I never did tell Carol about my dream, but somehow I think she knew. She never asked me what prompted me to call her and never exhibited any surprise. I guess it was just part of God's greater plan.

God truly gave me the strength to put aside my own agenda and go forward with love and forgiveness. Letting go of pain that someone has inflicted on you is not an easy task. Communication and above all honesty were the keys to breaking down the barriers that existed between us. Somehow Carol and I rebuilt a trust in one another, a trust we once had. By the grace of God, this trust was the key that allowed not only forgiveness but ultimately the gift of reconciliation. At this point I couldn't help but think of the Biblical story of the Prodigal Son.

I now believe that Carol and I will always have a bond that will never be broken. This bond is similar to that of a tattoo, something to be worn for eternity. Maybe our roles as Romeo and Juliet did have a bearing, a purpose after all. Even though we ventured off in different directions decades ago, our spiritual growth continued. And we did finally meet again. Yes, I did finally meet the girl from yesterday. No, I never got a chance to tell Carol my major issue, but it really didn't matter now. I was able to provide her the help she so desperately needed at this time in her life, and find peace and forgiveness in my own. We all experience hurt caused by others and no one can live a life unscathed. Forgiveness it seems, was the key to unlocking the door, the door that allowed me greater purpose and happiness in my life.

Sometimes we must learn to forgive ourselves before we have the courage to reach across the aisle to others. As

Carol said, life is fickle, full of twists and turns. Life does spin on a dime, and could have very easily gone differently for both of us. Somehow, as we weave our way, we must learn to accept God's will. I know in my heart that I have loved two women in my lifetime. To rank their loves would be a great disservice to God and his wonderful gift of love. The loves came at different times, each under its own unique circumstances. I thank the Lord for His wonderful gift of love.

The most important thing that I will take from this is that *I* was truly loved. What greater gift could we have. Years ago, someone once told me that many times God's most incredible gifts can not be seen or even touched. They must be felt. I have come a long way in a short period. No doubt I have grown in ways in which just a few short weeks ago, I didn't have any conception of. Stronger and wiser, I am now able to accept life's hand that I have been dealt. Life is complicated. God isn't. God does give us tomorrow to get better at what we do today. We must appreciate each and every experience we encounter. Coincidence? There is no such thing. Even when the encounter is a negative one, we must pick ourselves up and believe. God simply had another path for us, another path to His glory.

The trip to Milwaukee went quickly. I drove straight through as thoughts raced through my mind. As it turned out, I had an extra hour, so I took the exit and drove through our old town. The first thing I observed was the sign for the observation tower at the state park. I drove straight to the park where Carol and I had picnicked many times. From the parking lot I could see what appeared to be the very same picnic table where I had waited for Carol. That time thirty-eight years earlier had transfigured my life.

For a long moment I gazed, and then thanked the Lord for giving me the strength and resolve to find my path from that day to this one. That had been such a telling time in my life, and with God's strength I had come out stronger.

Finally, I drove down the road to Carol's old house. It looked the same—remarkably, even the exact same color. The driveway had not changed. I'm sure, however, its blacktop had been repaired numerous times.

I pulled into the driveway as if to change directions and go back. As I turned in, I stopped for a brief moment. I put the car in park, took a deep breath, closed my eyes, and sat back amid thoughts of all the wonderful conversations Carol and I had enjoyed right in this spot. It seemed strange. Just last night we had had similar ones in Carol's home in McGregor. It seemed that I now had gotten a chance to say goodbye not only to Carol, but to the special place where we had experienced the feeling of love for the first time. This place had defined not only her, but defined me as well. I thanked the Lord for my wonderful blessing and made my way back to the freeway.

Before I realized, it was already noon. The drive down I-94 went smoothly. In Milwaukee I grabbed a quick bite to eat and was at the client's office on the east side by 1:30 p.m. The meeting went well, and we wrapped up about 5:30.

The preliminary work I had done on their behalf served to help things run smoothly. I would be able to leave tomorrow morning, right on schedule. I went out to eat with their controller, Ernie, at a nice Italian restaurant at Bay Shore. Strangely, Ernie confided that he had just lost his mother to cancer a few weeks before. She had been only fifty-nine when she died. The cancer had progressed very quickly, in just six months she was gone. I could tell that he was still very distraught about the situation and had yet to come to grips with it. As we talked, he seemed to really open up to me, and I did my best to listen with understanding. I then remembered all the literature about grieving back in my suitcase in my room.

Being only a block from my motel, between dinner and dessert, I ran to my room and retrieved the information. Ernie was extremely happy to receive it. We talked about his joining a support group and the benefits it would bring. Once again, divine timing was perfect for me to help him.

Ernie told me how much he appreciated my help. "Boy, you guys really live up to your company motto, 'We don't only help businesses, we help people.' Don't you?"

"Ernie, we try our best."

No, I guess there is no such thing as coincidence. God does work in mysterious ways. I gave Ernie a hug goodbye. He, too, would be an honorary member of 'God's team.'

Back in my room I called Julie. She had been awaiting my call. It was great to hear her voice. She reminded me she would be at the airport tomorrow at 3:00 p.m. to pick me up.

As I settled into bed, I felt almost numb. I began to wonder how Carol was coping? That night I again dreamed of Carol. The colors of blue and yellow played prominently, along with thoughts of love, peace, joy, and happiness. When I awoke, though I wasn't quite sure, I thought I might have glimpsed her husband at the picnic table. However, I just wasn't sure. Ever since my very first dream, I had never been able to see him again.

My flight landed on time. Julie was waiting for me. I gave her a big hug and kiss and did not want to let her go. She could sense I was stressed, so as a treat she decided to stop at my favorite local restaurant, the AZ Sports Grill. Over a glass of wine before dinner, I gave her a play-by-play of my time in McGregor. I told her that Carol looked *great*, a comment she seemed to completely ignore. I told her a force was operating in all of this that I really couldn't explain. We discussed how my dream seemed to be coming true in every respect, and that I had been destined to make the trip. Too many things had fallen in place for this to be a coincidence. I reminded Julie of Jim's picture and told her about the footprints, the muddy sneakers.

After a moment, she inquired, "Was there anyone else around in the park?"

"No, I didn't see anyone," I replied.

Julie seemed to take everything in stride. The last few years as our children were on their own, we had truly grown as a couple. We seemed to be bonding in yet another way, one I had not thought even existed. Although it felt like a natural progression, it's timing and intensity at times felt surreal. Life's stages are truly another gift of God.

I thanked Julie for allowing me to take this trip and having so much faith and trust in me. I also mentioned something else. Ever since this dream episode had begun about eight weeks ago, I had been thinking more each day of making a life change. "I intend to look into working with people who are grieving," I said. 'These people are special in my heart. I get such a good feeling when the right words come out of my mouth and appear to make a difference. It's like the Lord is speaking through me."

Julie smiled. "Honey, that's so wonderful. I love you very much," she said.

We had a wonderful dinner and got to bed relatively early. Since tomorrow would be Saturday, we decided to sleep in and enjoy a nice, leisurely weekend together. I didn't realize how exhausted I really was. I dozed off immediately and slept straight through the night without dreaming at all—the first such time in nearly two months. Apparently I had finally run the course and had completed my mission.

It must have been around 5:00 a.m. when a large gust of wind blew the drape on our bedroom patio door. I woke momentarily to its sound, sat up in bed, then immediately fell back to asleep. I now dreamed of Carol again. This time she was at the picnic table with me. She smiled and said, "Jake, have you met my husband, Jim?" I looked across. The man with the dark complexion and the goatee smiled at me. Then he handed me the same silver box as he had four weeks earlier in Ms. Tarver's office. Its dimensions were the same.

I took the box from him. He smiled, gestured for me to open it. I could feel Carol's love and presence beside me as I removed the cover. I reached inside, again felt a piece of paper. Slowly I pulled the paper out, and now seemed to unfold it easily.

It was blank. Then I felt another rush—Carol's love, peace, joy, happiness—radiate my being. The paper began to turn yellow, and slight blue markings appeared across it. I felt another, even greater surge from Carol. At the same time I could feel tears streaming uncontrollably down my face. All at once, as if I were viewing the paper through a pair of binoculars and now focusing in, the words grew ever vibrant and clear. I felt love, peace, joy, and happiness more than I ever felt before in my entire life. I wiped the tears away, and began to read the message:

My Dearest One,

Love is God and God is love. It is the universal current which connects all. It is the wellspring of happiness. It is simple yet it is complex. Romantic love is but only one aspect. Real love is the ability to see and know that God is in everyone. God is our reason for being. He is all loving and has taught us how to love by example. Love is the answer. Love is the key. Love is real. It is everywhere, but one must open their eyes to see love. Most people miss it. It is right in front of them. When you see the goodness in someone or in a situation, you see love. It is the greatest force of the universe. It is wonderful and overwhelming at the same time. When you seek love, you find it. God's love allows us to become more than we ever thought possible.

We must not harden our hearts. One must break through the cold stone to find the truth. When the answers that are locked deep inside are found, so surfaces the truth. To truly understand one another, we must know where that person has been, what they have loved, how have they suffered and what they truly believe in. It is not easy to love someone that has harmed you. It is more difficult if that person is yourself. Forgiveness is the key to breaking through into a life of bliss and unending happiness. At the end of darkness is light. The light is love. You have come to the light my brother.

Every person and relationship has meaning and value. Each one provides insight for you to continue to grow in your ability to love unconditionally, like our Father loves each of us. Take the best from each relationship. Think of each relationship as a petal on a flower. One petal does not make a beautiful flower, but many petals create a work of beauty. Love often, love unconditionally, create a beautiful bouquet of love. In the end, each one of these flowers has a place in our Father's heavenly garden...the garden of paradise. The Garden of Love.

The beginning circles around to the end. The Garden of Eden is a real place. It is where love began. In the end, everyone will once again return to our Father's heavenly Garden where there will be eternal love, peace, joy, and happiness. Jake, I thank you for your generous gift of love. Your undertaking is now realized. Someday we will meet in the glory of the Father. Until then remember to love, love, love one another.

My peace I leave with you,

St. James

A slight tug came at my shoulder, amid Julie's voice. "Honey, are you all right? Jake, please—wake up."

I opened my eyes, looked her way.

"Jake you are crying–what's the matter?"

"Everything is fine. I was just dreaming again."

"And this time, Honey, you were talking in your sleep."

"I was? What did I say?"

"Jake, as plain as day you said—'*And also with you!*'"

Epilogue

All you dreamers who have the courage to follow your dreams, I applaud you. All you first loves who flourish in their time, appreciate the moments, remember the magic. Life holds many mysteries along the way. Among these is a force in nature that does not factor in time, logic, or certainty. This force lies deep within our souls and is available at our request. We need only summon its arrival and celebrate this wonderful gift from God.

I was extremely fortunate to be touched by this gift that would awaken me and push me in a new direction! Yes, this power aroused me and sent me back to a time of great passion in my life. This force spoke to me and told me there is a time to remember, a time to celebrate. This same energy that had earlier put Carol and me on separate paths had now reunited us. Maybe past loves don't come and go like the seasons. Maybe they exist in their own realms and are touched briefly each night by our unconscious selves. This moment of touch opens the door to our spiritual selves, allowing us to relive in detail these wonderful moments of love. Through this door we can receive messages and be armed with yet another gift— divine timing. How blessed was I to have received this gift in my life! God interceded through my dream and allowed me to not only help a dear friend, but receive lasting peace in my heart. This ultimately allowed me to heal through God's good grace. In less than two months my life had come full circle. Although God's path for me was much different than

I had originally planned, I could never be where am today without this detour. We must remember that God's ways are not our ways. Life's events transfigure us. God comes to us each day disguised as life. We must move ahead with the grace of God.

As I look back closely at my dreams, my connection it seemed was not entirely with Carol but with her husband of thirty-eight years. Jim and I had never met, but more importantly we had shared a significant characteristic, an eternal love of Carol. Somehow Jim had found a way to help Carol overcome her grief. He wanted her to be happy and continue to live life each day to the fullest. I believe that I was chosen for my task because Jim knew I truly did love Carol and would help her with all my heart. In addition, I believe he felt that my frustration in not being able to say goodbye early on would work in his favor. In return for my support, encouragement, and love, he found a way to reward me by placing lasting peace in my heart. His unconditional love of Carol is what made this *all* possible. I will never know for sure if the footprints and the muddy sneakers were Jim's doing, but I sure felt a presence that day. What I had originally thought was my shadow self and then my yogi just may have been an angel sent from heaven. I am now armed with a power of belief that gives me greater strength. However, I will not use this gift to delve more deeply into my soul. I will let life proceed in its own time and space and unfold for me day by day, gift by gift. Relationships, abundance, desires, ideas, and even dreams are all gifts from

God. We must be thankful for his gifts and trust in the path He has chosen for each one of us.

As I now think of Carol back in Iowa, I pray that she can accept her new path. I pray that she can find the peace in her heart and continue to praise the Lord. Now as I return to my normal routine, things will never be quite the same. With my renewed faith and love, I can now go forward with greater confidence. I am now content to appreciate Carol's essence and her love from a distance much like I did at the Legion Hall dance the first time I saw her. Just remember, if you don't understand your dreams don't worry—the Lord will make sure you understand just enough, and He will take care of the rest.

Although we lived relatively separate lives, I believe Carol and I developed a bond that will outlive both of our natural lives and exist in that special realm. Someday soon, perhaps for her sixtieth birthday, I will send her flowers. This will serve as a reminder for Carol to remember, to celebrate, and to believe in the power of God's love. I want to acknowledge just how far we have each come on our spiritual paths. After all, we are spirits having a human experience, not humans having a spiritual experience. I will inscribe a card for her on that special day that will proclaim, "To a life of love, peace, joy, and happiness. May God bless you, and always know that I love you." I will make sure it's written on yellow paper and inscribed with blue ink.

Amen.